CHEWING
the CUD

DICK KING-SMITH

CHEWING
the CUD

With drawings by
Harry Horse

VIKING

Published by the Penguin Group
Penguin Books Ltd, 27 Wrights Lane, London W8 5TZ, England
Penguin Putnam Inc., 375 Hudson Street, New York, New York 10014, USA
Penguin Books Australia Ltd, Ringwood, Victoria, Australia
Penguin Books Canada Ltd, 10 Alcorn Avenue, Toronto, Ontario, Canada M4V 3B2
Penguin Books India (P) Ltd, 11 Community Centre, Panchsheel Park,
New Delhi – 110 017, India
Penguin Books (NZ) Ltd, Cnr Rosedale and Airborne Roads, Albany, Auckland,
New Zealand
Penguin Books (South Africa) (Pty) Ltd, 5 Watkins Street, Denver Ext 4,
Johannesburg 2094, South Africa

On the World Wide Web at: www.penguin.com

Penguin Books Ltd, Registered Offices: Harmondsworth, Middlesex, England

First published 2001
1

The moral right of the author and illustrator has been asserted

Set in 11/16pt Sabon

Printed in England by Clays Ltd, St Ives plc

British Library Cataloguing in Publication Data
A CIP catalogue record for this book is available from the British Library

ISBN 0–670–89964–X

For Myrle

CONTENTS

What's in a Name?

Children often ask me if the name under which I write is my real one. I say 'Yes', but it's not strictly true. Though everybody calls me 'Dick', my real name, I must confess, is Gordon and, when I was small, everyone called me that. Indeed, my grandparents always did.

I hated the name.

I was christened Ronald Gordon, the first name after Father, the second after some South African who had been a pal of his in the Great War and became one of my two godfathers. I never met the man, never heard from him and, from an early age, disliked his name. My other godfather, Ivor Nicholson, a publisher, always sent me a ten-pound note on my birthday, so I should probably have been quite happy to be named 'Ivor'.

I don't know quite why I took against the name Gordon so much. There is, I suppose, nothing much wrong with it (apologies to any so-called who are reading this) but I just plain didn't like it and, when I went to prep school, I managed quickly to acquire the nickname of Bertie. How? Why? Don't know. But at some point when I was quite small, I was walking down the lane from our house with my nanny, Ethel, and I fell and grazed my knee. The story goes that in order for my nanny not to see my tears, I pointed up into the sky and said, 'Look at the dicky-birds!' After that, Mother and Father used on occasion to call me 'Dicky-bird', which then shrank to Dicky, and eventually to plain 'Dick'. Put together with 'King' and 'Smith', a trio of ugly sounds results, but I've got used to it over the years, though I suppose it would have been nice to have, as an author, a really mellifluous name that tripped off the tongue, like David Dearlove, or Oliver Grandfield.

Children who write to me often have difficulty with the hyphen between the two parts of my surname, and almost always address me as Dick-King-Smith just to be on the safe side. Once I even had a letter beginning 'Dear-Dick-King-Smith'.

My surname was the result of various Kings marrying various Smiths, or indeed Smiths marrying Kings. By chance also, an exploration of my family tree undertaken by my Great-uncle Oswald, a keen amateur genealogist, led back to another King, none other than Charles II. Quite possibly most people in England are related to King Charles II, 'the Black Boy', a libertine of the first order, who fathered so many children on the wrong side of the blanket. I am descended from a Lady Russell who bore the king a daughter. This line then descended for a while on the distaff side until eventually one of my female ancestors married a Mr King (or Smith, not sure which).

Great-uncle Oswald, incidentally, was so shocked by the discovery of the original bastardy that he went into a decline and passed away.

Charles II's genes must have been pretty strong. For almost a couple of centuries after his death there is a story in the family that another ancestor of mine, John James Smith, emigrated to the USA and, in New York State, founded the Mormons. He was eventually murdered, but not before he had married no less than thirty-three wives.

Chapter 1

THE SHEEP-PIG

1 July
Dominion Day (Canada)
The village fête. In charge of Guess-the-Weight-of-the-Pig.

In late 1995, my wife, Myrle, and I walked into a London cinema to see a film called *Babe*. We had no idea what to expect.

Eight years or more had gone by since I had sold the world rights of a book of mine, *The Sheep-Pig*, to an Australian company, and I knew nothing at all about their adaptation of Book into Film.

True, I had been asked – by the big Hollywood studio, Universal Pictures of America, who were putting up the money – if I would like to see something of the production, but after I had said, 'Yes, please, so long as I don't have to step on board an aeroplane', I heard nothing more.

We took our seats. The opening credits came up on the huge screen. Among them:

ADAPTED FROM THE BOOK
BY
DICK KING-SMITH

We nudged each other.

Myrle and I sat enthralled throughout the film. It was soon plain to us that the adaptation from the book had been wonderfully well done.

There were differences, of course – there always are when you change something from one medium to another. There were additional pieces of action, and quite an array of new characters – another dog, the cat, that marvellous duck – but the director had stuck pretty faithfully to the central theme of my original story: the tale of an orphaned piglet who is adopted by a farmer and by his sheep-dog. This little pig, by virtue of his intelligence and determination, by his courage, and especially through his realization that politeness pays, comes eventually to win the Grand Challenge Sheep-dog Trials. One particular thing about the film that delighted me was that, as soon as I set eyes on the actor who played Farmer Hogget, I saw to my amazement that he was the spitting image of the imaginary figure I'd had in my head when I wrote the book all those years before.

I've seen *Babe* six times now and every time I've laughed and I've cried, but of course at that first viewing we had no idea that the film would become such a huge international success. During the many years that it was in the making, I'd written masses of other children's books since *The Sheep-Pig*, but that was to be the one that would bring me so much publicity and do me such a lot of good.

If you were to ask me to choose a favourite from among the dozens and dozens of books I've produced, I would probably say I think it may be the best.

It's always nice for me to think that, in a funny way, *Babe* was born here, in the little village where we live. I mean that he was born in my head, in my imagination, thanks to our annual village Summer Fête.

One particular year I was in charge of the Guess-the-Weight-of-the-Pig stall, and I must, I suppose, have thought as I stood upon the village green, recording people's guesses and taking their money, that it was a shame that such a lovely little pink pig should end up, once he was big enough, in the deep-freeze.

Suppose fate had something quite different in store for him? Suppose he should go and live on a farm, with a sheep-dog as his foster-mother? Suppose he should want to do what she did?

He couldn't be a sheep-dog.
But he could be a sheep-pig.

For twenty years and more I have come to think of myself as a writer. But for all the early part of my life I thought of myself as a farmer and, indeed, between 1947 and 1967, I was one.

Often, in my dreams, we are still at our first farm, Woodlands Farm. The children are still small (though in fact one of them now has a grandchild about the same age).

Occasionally in these dreams, I drive a tractor or work in a remembered field, but I am more likely to be in the farm buildings, preparing food in the old disused pigsty, feeding the pigs in the barn or the calves in the stables or the hens in the loft or the rabbits in a loose-box. Woodlands Farm was like that – everything lived in an unexpected place. Mostly, of course, I'm in the cowshed, doing the milking, always somehow seeming to be behindhand, I'm late, I'll never be finished in time for the milk lorry, get a move on, do.

For Myrle and me, that first farm was a bit like the toy farms that each of us had played with as small children. It was stocked with practically every sort of animal you could think of. It was a bit of a muddle, but a cosy muddle. It was full of interest, then in reality, now in dreams.

Chapter 2

FARMHAND

*'Can you tell me if any there be
That will give me employ,
To plough and sow, and reap and mow,
And be a farmer's boy?'*

I think I always wanted to farm. I would have had an idealized picture of the life, I suppose, but the wish had two strong roots: to continue to live in the country and to work with animals. It was all going to be so simple. The pets that I had always kept, the rabbits, the guinea-pigs, the fancy mice and rats, the ornamental pheasants, the budgerigars, would translate into cattle and pigs and poultry.

When I was eighteen, I determined to make a start,

unconcerned that I was by nature unbusinesslike, that anything mechanical baffled me, and that my educational qualifications for the job were ten years of studying the classics. 'How blest beyond all blessings are farmers,' Virgil had said, '... far from the clash of arms.'

In Europe the clash had begun. In Wiltshire, I took my first steps on the road that was to lead, seven years later, to Woodlands Farm. 'They won't call you up for a year or so,' my father said, 'so you can either go up to Cambridge in that time, or you can go and do some practical work on a farm.' I jumped at that. I certainly didn't want to join the Army till I had to, nor, newly released from schooling, did I want to go to university. But farming – now, that's what I'd long wanted to do. Father would find a farmer who was willing to take me as a pupil and would pay him the necessary premium. He found one in the Wylye Valley in Wiltshire, and there I went in the early summer of 1940. Mother sent me tin boxes of 100 Players Medium cigarettes. My employer gave me a pound a week. And I worked hard.

I spent the first four back-breaking blistering weeks at Tytherington Farm hand-hoeing a huge field of sugar-beet. The seemingly endless rows of young plants had to be cleared and singled. The weather was right and every available man was at it. At first I scratched about as clumsily as a newly hatched chick in a barnyard, but gradually they showed me how to use the hoe, to push with it as well as pull, to tease out and deftly flick aside the competing weeds, to cut and scrape and twist the wrist to take away all the surplus seedlings at one spot, a deft instant selection of the fittest that left only the master plant standing to grow to beet's estate. Each completed row had eventually to be a rigidly dressed, exactly spaced rank of the élite, chosen on merit from that great army of plants.

At the start of each pass across the field, at the headland, we are level — the five farm labourers, the horseman and me. There are others on the farm, of course. There are the four poultry men, already gone up to the downs to tend many thousands of birds in fold units; they stand like charioteers in their little rubber-tyred tumbrils pulled by an assortment of strange ponies and broken-winded hunters. And the foreman, a dour Yorkshireman called Howard, is up there too with his hairy dog, Bran, to tend the sheep and the big mobs of Irish-bred stirk heifers running with their bulls. And there are tractor-drivers at work somewhere, far out of earshot. But the hoeing gang is the usual one of Albie Ball and Billy Ball and Tom Smith and Fred Smith called Henry to distinguish him from the fifth, Fred Prince. And Jack Stannard the horseman, roped in to help and grumbling at it. And me.

By the time we've been going for a bit, things look rather different. Albie, in keeping with his undefined but acknowledged position of leadership among the men, is clearly the best man in the field. Tall body bent, blue eyes sharp in a very red face, the hoe flicking in his hands like a striking snake, he is some yards ahead of Tom, Henry and Fred. Of these three, Tom has the edge in speed, but deliberately handicaps himself, slowing his work by much chat and laughter. Then comes Albie's uncle, Billy, a very small man with a drooping moustache and a high voice, broader than any in his speech. He seems to me to be extremely old (he might have been in his fifties) and shouts ahead to keep in with the conversation. Behind him comes Jack with his limp – some mettlesome horse had once smashed him against a wall – and a look of distaste at unaccustomed fieldwork. And last of course is the beginner.

But Albie, as soon as he reaches the far headland, turns and comes back up one or another's unfinished row, and so do the others in their turn, so that we all start again together, seven rows of sugar-beet nearer to the other, far distant side of the field.

They were very good to me, those farm men. They showed a lot of patience when I made a mess of a job, and they were always willing to teach me how to do a thing right. These days machinery reigns and there is almost always a tractor with something on its front or back end to do the donkey work. But then we were usually on our flat feet, holding a hoe or a fork or a rake, spade, pickaxe, crowbar, sledgehammer, beetle, billhook, reaphook, slasher

– the list is endless, and there's a right and a wrong way to handle each.

For hay or straw you must master the pitchfork, the 'two-grain prong' they call it in Wiltshire. There are parallels with the game of golf, where the same club in different hands may send the ball flying long and true or scuttling feebly to hide itself in the rough for shame. Success lies in the timing, the grip, the stance, the swing, the unhurried rhythm. So it is in the hayfield.

'Yur, look at old Dick. Wass doing then, stabbing Germans?'

'Thee'll 'ave it droo thy vut if thee dussn't watch out.'

'Thee 'on't pick up no more nor a bird's nest like that.'

'Give us thic prong, Dick. Now lookzee …' And Albie or Tom or Henry would tease and twirl and cajole a great mass of hay into place, and then, leaning over the top of it, lance the two slim forward-facing tines into the exact magical kernel of the heap. A shift of the grip, a downward press with the right hand at the very end of the long shaft, a lift with the low-gripping left hand, an easy twist and heave, and a dip of the shoulders to bring the prong upright, and there's a miniature haystack walking away towards the wagon. It's not as easy as it looks.

In the nature of things, I improved. And in the course of time I began to learn how to do a whole host of things I'd never done before. How to stook corn and how to pitch sheaves up on to a wagon, and thence to the rick-maker high on the rick or mow. How to lift and carry sacks of wheat as heavy as myself. How to harness and drive a horse in shafts. How to dig a post-hole and hang a gate and strain a four-strand wire fence, and throw a ewe on her back for the shearers, and fling dung, and drive cattle, and cut a block of hay from the mow with a hay-knife.

I began to make myself useful, to stockman or shepherd, to carter or thatcher, in the hayfield, at harvest, or by the threshing machine. Here I was usually condemned to be 'on the dust' – responsible for raking away and heaping aside the dirty powdery choking river of chaff and bristly awns and weed seeds and general rubbish that the roaring heaving monster voided from its bowels, filling eyes, ears, mouth and nostrils, penetrating up sleeves and trouser legs and down collars, ferreting in through the very lace holes of my boots.

I learned other things too, for example, to enjoy smoking and drinking. As well as Mother's Players, there were those yellow packets of Star or the green of

Woodbines, five for twopence, and evenings in the Bell or the Wheatsheaf.

'Wass going to have then, Dick? We'm on the cider.'

'Oh thanks, Tom. Just a half.'

Or more. It was the hard stuff, the rough. And of course they egged me on. And I learned a bit about swearing. Billy Ball, especially, was a master swearer. Perhaps it was because he was so small and toothless and squeaky-voiced that the younger ones made a butt of him. Mind you, it was teasing, not taunting, and he liked it.

'Where bist going Satdy, then, Billy?'

'Going in to town, young Henry, going in to town.' (Billy mostly said things twice. 'Town' was Warminster.)

'Don'ee go down such and such a street then.'

'Why not, young Henry, why not?'

'Thee might get accosted, 'sno.' ('Sno' or 'eesno' equals 'dost thou know' or 'do you know'.)

'Costed? Wass mean, costed?'

''Tis chock vull of prostitutes down there, Billy.'

'Prostitutes, eh, young Henry? That don't frighten old Billy, not frighten old Billy it don't.' And Billy would become, or appear to become, very excited, leaping about and gesticulating wildly.

'I'll show they tarts, young Henry. I'll show they!'

'Wass going to show 'em, Billy?'

'Old Billy'll show they a thing or two!'

'Thee's never got two, Billy, hast?'

And so it would go on, with Billy's bawdiness breaking new records as with many foul oaths he outlined his new-found intentions towards the whores of Warminster, while Henry and Fred and Tom rolled about in delight, and Albie beamed proudly down on his bantam-cock of an uncle.

It was Billy Ball who was run away with one day in harvest time, and thinking about that reminds me how big a part the horse still played, sixty years ago. There were tractors of course: an early Fordson, a Case, an International, a green John Deere and an orange Allis Chalmers. It was a big farm and already the downs as well as the lower lands were being ploughed and cultivated and sown to grow food for a nation at war. But the bulk of the wagons and carts still had shafts to them, not drawbars, and there was work for horses in a dozen other ways – harrowing, horse-hoeing, hay-raking, for example.

Indeed in the hayfield, where the pick-up baler was only just beginning to show its face, we used a monstrous horse-operated Canadian machine to lift the loose hay up on to the mow. First the hay was pushed up together, not by tractors, but by a couple of ancient and aristocratic motor cars fitted with wooden sweeps, a Lea-Francis and a Lagonda. Then, once a sufficient mountain of hay had been collected, Jack would whip up the horses – four there were abreast – and somehow (the mechanics of the thing are quite beyond me) this great contraption, a cross between a giant's toast-rack and a Roman ballista, would creak and crack and groan and throw half a wagonload up on to the top of the mow in one convulsive heave.

Every day started among the horses, for first thing in the morning Howard the foreman gave his orders in the stables. In the gloom of the long narrow building, a barred window at either end, he would stand with one arm thrown over a huge shining bottom, and allot the different jobs to be done, depending on weather and season. And the air was a marvellous mixture of the smells of hay and leather and dung and just plain horse, and the sounds were of soft snortings and bubbly blowings through velvet lips and now and then the stamp of a heavy hoof on the cobbled floor.

We would stand facing that long row of backsides, which were of several sizes and of many colours, for they were a motley lot at Tytherington Farm. Some, like the motor cars, had known better times – two or three heavy hunters and one animal with a bit of blood in him, who had had to forget their palmier days and mingle with a lower class of person; halfway horses with hairy heels and common features. The poultrymen especially had strange beasts to pull their light loads – like Ginger, a rawboned chestnut with a lot of yellow teeth (very like her namesake in *Black Beauty* for 'the ears were laid back and the eye looked rather ill-tempered'), and a kind of outsize pony called Pony, who could trot at lightning speed despite having very short legs, and sported a forelock that completely covered its face. The queen of them all to my mind was Flower, a purebred Shire mare. The only one to look the part, she dwarfed the rest.

Outside the stables, there were horses all over the place. The farmer and his wife hunted with the Wylye Valley, and there were always a number of fine animals turned out up on the downs in the off-season. And in an orchard behind the farm buildings there lived a strange assortment of very old pensioners – one mare was reputed to be forty-five years of age. And with them three gaunt mules, survivors of an eight-mule team that had done the ploughing of the farm in the early twenties. Despite their impotence they dreamed vain dreams of virility and leaped upon the ancients with loud pretentious brays.

Most of the working horses were quirky beasts, each with its own pet phobia. Alice, for example, half-Shire half-something and a sprightly thirty-eight, was totally trustworthy in traffic but terrified of gateposts. Driving Alice through a gateway, which might occur many times a day, was something to be done with maximum concentration and a firm hold of the reins. She had to be steered exactly between the posts – fearful monsters as you could see by her pricked ears, braced neck and rolling eyes. They were waiting, she knew, to do her a terrible mischief, and if you should touch a careless wheel against one as you went through, Alice was off, no matter what the load, straight into a gallop that would have done justice to a two-year-old.

The great Flower had one *bête noire* (she was green, in fact) and that was a beast even larger than herself – the local bus. And her reaction was not to bolt but to buck. At sight of the approaching titan, she would throw herself against the breeching, tossing her head, whinnying, and paddling madly at the ground with her huge soup-plate hoofs, the frenzy increasing as the bus drew nearer. Better to be in an empty Scotch cart than a loaded four-wheel wagon when the giants met.

And then there was Foxianna. She was a liver chestnut mare with rusty mane and tail, who had served her time in the hunting field and was as biddable as you could wish. Until she saw a pig. Pigs to her were devils incarnate, and even the smell or the distant sound of them was enough to give her the vapours.

I drove her in a hay-rake once, sitting contentedly in the iron seat as we swept up the rakings in a roadside field. The sun was shining, the mare plodded along sensibly, and I had learned to make her stop and start and turn, and to work the machine, leaving neat rollers of hay at regular intervals. But, though there were no pigs on Tytherington Farm, there was a herd of Saddlebacks on the land beyond the road and, as we made a turn at the headland nearest to it, there they were, dozens of them, big ones and small ones, staring through the fence at us with malevolent little eyes.

'Pi-i-i-i-igs!' screamed Foxianna, or that's what it sounded like. And in one violent crashing movement she lunged backwards, digging the long curved tines into the ground and sending me shooting out over the back, and then she was gone like the wind with the hay-rake bouncing and clanging behind her flying ginger tail.

So I was run away from, but it was Billy Ball who was run away with. We had been picking up a field of wheat. The combine, or harvester-thresher as it was at first called, was beginning to be used in English cornfields, but the old reaper-and-binder was still the principal machine at work. The cut corn stood in shocks or stooks, each of ten sheaves, stacked four against four with one to close each end off, their butts to the ground, their heads upright to catch the air and dry the moisture in the grain. Then, in time, they were loaded on to wagons and carried to the corn mow, built on a layer of brushwood – a 'stavel' by name – to keep the bottom layers from the ground. And there the wheat or barley or oats stayed, secure under a roof of thatch, until threshing time after the turn of the year.

This particular piece, of twenty or thirty acres I think, was of level downland and the spot chosen for the mow convenient; ideal therefore for the big four-wheeled horse-drawn wagons with their wooden 'ladders' at either end, and in particular for the biggest of them all, that we called the Queen Mary, so enormous that no one but Flower was ever put to it, and even she could only pull it part-loaded. For a full load a trace horse was needed as well, and that day Albie was certainly building them full. With set weather, a dry flat ground, two of us pitching up on either side, and Billy up on the load to feed him, I wouldn't like to guess how many layings of long-strawed heavy-headed wheat sheaves Albie built on the deck of the Queen Mary.

At last, from the top of the mountain, he said, 'That'll do.' Tom stuck his prong into the side of the load for Albie to grasp in his descent, and down he slid.

'Bist coming down, Uncle Billy?'

'I'll ride in to the mow, my dear, I'll ride in to the mow,' piped Billy, perched almost out of sight on the summit. But there was a fly in the ointment, or rather in the hot August air, that changed the whole idyllic scene in a flash. One moment the horses were standing quietly, waiting for the order to move on – Flower in the shafts and in the traces a much smaller but very strong and muscular animal, a bay horse called Mac – and the next they were all of a fidget, for though we could not, they could hear the gadfly's thin metallic whine. And then it struck.

It must have stung Mac, for before anyone could get to his head he shot forward in one great galvanic bound, dragging Flower into her collar. And in terror she began to trundle and immediately, it seemed, they were at the gallop, the Queen Mary sailing behind them, and on top of her, little Billy, flat on his belly, hanging on with every finger and toe.

If the field had been even bigger it might have all ended happily as the horses tired. As it was, Mac ran slap into a five-strand barbed-wire fence and burst it. The pain of it brought him up short, and Flower executed an elephantine sort of swerve to miss him, and the Queen tipped up on to two wheels. Over went Albie's enormous load and down came Billy.

It could have been worse. Flower was all right, and Mac, though he was terribly cut all across his legs and broad chest, had suffered no irreparable harm and mended in due course. But at the time it was Billy we were worried about as we dashed up, convinced that a fall on to hard ground at speed from that height must have broken something, a leg maybe, possibly his scrawny neck.

And then we heard, coming from within that great pile of fallen sheaves, the familiar tones, even shriller than usual, and the familiar language, infinitely worse than ever, and out he popped like a little polecat. And seeing that he was all in one piece we laughed till we cried. And the harder we laughed, the worse he swore.

I wouldn't put it past Billy Ball to be alive today, even though he'd have to be about a hundred and ten. But all the horses are long gone, and no hoof rings upon the cobblestones of the stables.

It was cold steel that ended my apprenticeship on Tytherington Farm. We were threshing barley at the side of a field called the Pig Ground (don't listen, Foxianna, I always thought). Excused, for once, being on the dust, I had been up in the pitch-hole of the straw-rick, feeding the sheaves to Albie. And when he had finished topping, I jumped down on to the wagon bed so that he could fill in the hole. Somebody, carelessly, had left a two-grain prong leaning against the side of the wagon, points up, and as I swung off the bed to the ground one tine went clean through my leg between the bone and the Achilles tendon, and stuck out four inches clear the other side.

I can't say it hurt that much going in but it did coming out. Albie stood behind me and locked his arms round my chest, and Tom and Henry laid hold of the handle. And it was one, two, three, heave, and goodbye to the Wylye Valley.

I didn't see Tytherington again for five years. Caesar may just have come and seen and conquered. I went abroad and fought and came home full of holes. But that's a very different story.

Chapter 3

MYRLE AND THE WAR

Who know no doubts or fears!
Then sing tow, row, row, row, row, row,
The British Grenadiers.

Now let's go back a little bit in time. By the end of
1936 I had spent four years at my prep school,
Beaudesert Park in the Cotswolds, and had just completed
my first two terms at Marlborough.

I spent a lot of my school holidays with Jamie and his
sister Margaret, who lived just up the lane from me. We
called ourselves the Red Hand Gang, a title whose blood-
thirstiness was unwarranted, since all we did was to play
endless card games or board games or, mostly, to wander

around the countryside in a carefree way that no parents these days could possibly allow. The gang's name came from the initiation ceremony (each scratched a finger with a pin and mingled the blood with that of the others) and certain tests had to be passed such as leaping across ditches or climbing trees. My brother Tony was admitted when he reached the age of four or so, but with easier requirements (narrower ditches, shorter trees, no bloodshed).

On Christmas Day 1936, something happened that was to affect the whole of the rest of my life and, in due course, a large number of other lives.

I had been given an air rifle as a Christmas present and was trying it out, firing out of an upstairs window at the trunk of the old crab-apple tree on the other side of the lawn, when, to my annoyance, I was required to stop and be introduced to a strange girl.

Mother and Father always had a large number of people, family and friends, for drinks on Christmas morning, and on this particular morning a couple who had recently moved into the district came with their two daughters. I didn't take much notice of the elder dark-haired one, she was sixteen for goodness' sake, and of no interest to someone of my age. But the younger one was fourteen, like me, and she didn't look too bad as girls went. She had fair hair and large brown eyes and wasn't giggly or silly like most girls.

More importantly, it turned out that she bred

budgerigars, which interested me, since I also did, in an aviary where I kept different-coloured birds all together, breeding quite indiscriminately – greens, yellows, various sort of blues, resulting in some very odd shades. Whereas this girl, so she gave me to understand, kept the various colours in separate flights, so that each bred true.

Her name, I found out, was Myrle England. Myrle's mother's family had lived in India at some time, and the unusual spelling of her name (to rhyme with 'girl') had been found on a gravestone at Naini Tal.

We seemed to have quite a lot of things in common, especially a liking for animals. I had rabbits and tortoises and guinea-pigs and mice and rats, but at that time I didn't have a dog of my own. Myrle did, a bull-terrier called Sally, whom she had trained to do some clever things. If a door was left open, Sally would shut it on command by jumping up and pushing at it with her forefeet. She would also use those feet to 'play' the piano, sitting up on the stool and producing loud crashing discords.

Over the next year or so, Myrle and I met a number of times, in the kind of uncomplicated relationship that children of that age have and, once, the two families went on holiday at the same time to the same place. We played golf too, where I could show off by driving the ball twice as far as she could (though seldom in the right direction). One thing annoyed me though. We had a competition, throwing stones from the bank into the big pond that fed water to the paper mills, and I was very miffed to find that she could throw further than I could.

I can't remember being heartbroken when Myrle's father changed his job and the England family moved away up into the Midlands. But I told myself that there was no girl I liked better.

We did not actually meet again until I had left Marlborough and was working on that Wiltshire farm. In the summer of 1940, when I was eighteen and she nearly so, I had a letter from her. I wrote back, hoping that perhaps we could meet again, and I suppose our respective mothers must have liaised about this. I had lodgings in Sutton Veny, and if Myrle were to come all the way from London to visit, then patently she would have to stay a night or two and, equally patently, the parents considered, she must be properly chaperoned. They were confident that my landlady, Mary Elliott, was just the person for such a job, and so very soon I found myself taking the bus into Warminster and then standing, waiting, outside the railway station.

Shall I recognize her, I thought? She will have changed after all, it's been two years or more. Then out through the station doors she came. Once we had been much the same in height, but now I was a head taller. Her fair hair had been worn short, now it hung in a blonde page-boy style. Her big brown eyes were the same, but her face – what had happened to it? Much, much later she told me that she was worried about blushing – on just such an occasion as that reunion, perhaps – and someone (well-meaning, who knows?) had recommended that she use a certain kind of face-powder, formulated to conceal blushes. It was a greenish powder. So there was I, confronted by this glamorous green-faced girl wearing a rather striking white-belted mackintosh with large lapels and epaulettes.

I imagine we shook hands. I suppose that in due course I offered to carry her suitcase to the bus. I know that we talked all the way back to Sutton Veny – so much had happened to each of us since our last meeting – and during her stay we went for long walks and talked a lot more and laughed at the same sort of jokes and generally got on very well together. A great deal of the talk was about animals: our dogs and other pets, the farm animals, wild animals. When the visit was over and I had left her at the railway station, I rang mother and told her roundly that I was going to marry Myrle one day.

There was to be one more meeting before we were both in uniform. This was in Devon, where her mother and sister Pam had taken a holiday cottage. This meeting, like the other, ended at a railway station, Taunton in fact, where I took a train north to Bristol and she went east to London. And for each of us it was this time a painful parting, neither wanting to leave the other.

In the summer of 1941, having decided that it was high time I joined up (I didn't want to wait to be conscripted, I wanted to volunteer), I said goodbye to family and friends, took the bus to Bath and thence the train to Devizes where the Wiltshires' Regimental Depot was. I reported myself at the gates to a sergeant who was everything that sergeants should be – full-chested, straight-backed, moustached, fierce-eyed, loud-mouthed. Then occurred the following conversation.

Self: 'Please. I've come to join up.'

Sergeant: 'Five and seven, or nine and eleven?'

Self (thinking 'Heavens, does he mean years?'): 'I just want to join up for the duration of the war.'

Sergeant (scornfully): 'We don't take duration soldiers in this regiment, sonny. You have to sign for a regular term.'

Self: 'Oh, well, thanks. Goodbye.'

And off I marched back to Devizes Station and caught the next train for Bath, and thence the next bus home. There was no one about as I walked up the drive. My younger brother, Tony, was away at school and Mother and Father were not as yet sitting with their evening drinks under the big horse-chestnut outside the drawing-room window. I climbed to the top of the tree and waited. Not long afterwards, they came out of the house and sat down in their chairs, Mother with a gin and tonic, Father with a pink gin. He lit his pipe, and she took from a case the first of many cigarettes, and they began to wonder aloud about their elder son, gone that day to take the King's shilling. Then, at some noise in the chestnut's leafy top, they looked up to see him climbing down.

Later that summer, I found out that the Brigade of Guards would accept duration enlistment (provided the volunteer was not too short) and I enlisted, as a Recruit, in the Grenadier Guards and was sent off to the Guards' Depot at Caterham.

Myrle enlisted in the WAAF some months before I joined the Army, and was, in due course, commissioned before I was. She ended up at Fighter Command at Stanmore as a filterer, and once I took a train from Windsor to meet her. I don't remember that the Guardsman saluted the pilot officer as he should have done, but I do recall that because of my lowly rank, I was not allowed into the Officers' Mess at Stanmore, and we had to say goodbye outside the gates of Fighter Command.

Looking back, it seems that at that time, the autumn of 1942, each of us had privately decided that we should get married, though this was never voiced. In fact, I never proposed to Myrle in formal fashion. One day she had come down from Stanmore to visit me at Windsor (I too was now commissioned) and we walked beside the Thames and then went to a riverside pub. There I said, 'I suppose it would be a good idea to be married, wouldn't it?' And she said, 'Yes.' So plans began.

Both of us were under age – twenty-one was the start of adulthood in those days – and so we needed, each of us, parental consent. Mother, Father and Myrle's mother were all agreeable, despite our youth. After all, we'd known each other such a time that there was little point in a long engagement, and before long I was sure to be posted abroad, so the sooner the wedding could be arranged the better. Though each of them, Father especially, must have considered the chances of our marriage being a short one. Many young front-line infantry soldiers did not live – as Father had only just managed to do – to tell the tale.

Myrle's father was a slightly different proposition, for he was abroad, a Group-Captain in the RAF, stationed in Egypt. Though he knew me of course, as a boy at any rate, he was less enthusiastic about the need for haste and said that he thought we should have an engagement of at least six months. Thankfully, one way or another, he was overridden and we were married from my parents' house on 6 February 1943.

Because we were so young, we had not yet made many friends, so the guests were mainly composed of relations – mostly mine – and old friends of my mother's and father's. Three of my brother officers in the Grenadiers were there, and Jamie, one-time second-in-command of the Red Hand Gang, stood best man to me.

Father had somehow laid in ample supplies of wine – a difficult thing to do in those wartime days – and everyone drank to what some of them must have thought of as 'those two children marrying'. So much so that two women, who had taken an instant dislike to one another, sat opposite at a table and let rip like fishwives.

Brother Tony, just turned fifteen, lay under the table (he'd had his share of wine) and listened as the names of various members of the animal kingdom were bandied above him: 'Stupid cow!', 'Silly bitch!', 'Making a pig of yourself!', 'How catty can you be?'. Next there was a thump, and Tony, lifting the edge of the tablecloth, was treated to the sight of the two women wrestling on the floor.

Then at last the local taxi took us away to Bath, where for the first time in our joint experience of railway stations, we rode off together on the puffer-train. To Warminster, in fact, and then by taxi to Sutton Veny and Home Farm once more and our kind ex-chaperone Mary and her husband, Ted, though this time we were not put in separate bedrooms. It wasn't a very long honeymoon – forty-eight hours was all each of us could get – but a little later we managed nine days' leave, which was spent at the Anchor at Porlock Weir on the Somerset coast, and we walked on Exmoor.

But time was fleeting and before long I was on embarkation leave, to be posted overseas with a number of Grenadier officers. Myrle was given compassionate leave to come down to Windsor and stay, at the Castle Hotel.

Then at last came yet another railway station scene. I remember with the most painful clarity, leaning out of the window of a compartment filled with friends all excited to some degree at the prospect before them – as young men are before they learn what war's all about – and kissing my new wife goodbye and seeing this small solitary figure walking away down the platform of Windsor Station and not looking back, resolutely not looking back. I must have thought, will I ever see her again?

It was to be eighteen months before I did.

First there was a long troopship voyage round the Cape of Good Hope and up the Red Sea to Egypt. Then a long drive westwards along the Mediterranean shore of Africa, to Tripoli, a journey that was to end with saying goodbye to a large number of chameleons that I'd collected *en route* – I didn't think they'd be too keen to accompany me on the invasion of Italy, which is what we were about to do.

We landed at Salerno, south of Naples, in early September of 1943, and slowly fought our way northwards. There were a lot of casualties, of course. Many men in my platoon were killed or wounded and, among the young officers of the battalion, I lost many friends. But apart from being frightened stiff a lot of the time, I was unscathed, even managing to miss one particular battle at Monte Camino, or Murder Mountain as it became known, where the casualties were terribly high. I was tucked up in bed in a Naples hospital with jaundice.

We fought slowly on northwards, the Germans defending each position bravely so that in the mountainous terrain there was never any chance of a breakthrough. Then, at last, after eleven months of active service, I met my Waterloo (just south of Florence).

We were dug in among the trees of a hilltop wood, my platoon and that of my friend Charlie. Charlie was sent off on a patrol, leaving me supposedly looking after both platoons. At around 5 a.m. the Germans suddenly put down a heavy barrage on us, so that there seemed to be shells bursting everywhere around us as we huddled in our slit trenches. Suddenly the stonk was over and in came the German attack, mounted, I learned much later, by men of the Storm Battalion of the Hermann Goering Division, very violent men armed with small rocket guns and a flame-thrower.

The flame-thrower was the first thing I saw, about ten yards in front of me. Luckily it misfired, spilling out a pitiable flame not six feet long, and before its operator could repair the thing, one of my Bren gunners shot him dead. I was by now standing behind a tree, shooting at the enemy with my German pistol, when suddenly I saw clearly that the hand-grenade that had just been lobbed at me was a British one, a thirty-six grenade, what used to be called a Mills bomb. I had this split second of seeing the thing clearly, as at cricket a fielder might see a skied ball on its way to him. I've always supposed that when Charlie went off on his patrol that night his men had left some grenades ready primed and the men of the Storm Battalion of course made use of them.

This one would certainly have killed me had it not been for my good old tree, which must have taken a lot of the blast, but anyway the grenade still did me a good deal of damage – leg, bottom, tummy. And though strangely I don't remember feeling much pain, no doubt because of shock, I do recall being very frightened that I would be left, lying helpless, to the tender mercies of those violent Germans. I cried out, as loudly as I could, 'This position will be defended to the last man and the last round!' just like something out of a *Boys' Own* story.

Over fifty years later, in Australia, to which he had emigrated, I met once again my platoon sergeant, Bill Grandfield, and in a Sydney pub he told me, 'When I saw you lying there bleeding, I went berserk!'

He had stood over my body blasting away with his tommy gun, and the rest of my platoon let rip too. Once the stretcher-bearers had carted me off, Bill was in fact in command of both my platoon and Charlie's and he held off the enemy for nearly a couple of hours till reinforcements arrived. He was, I'm glad to say, awarded the Military Medal. We had eight others wounded besides myself. The attackers, it was later found in the diary of one of them who had been taken prisoner, picked up twenty-six of their own dead.

I won't weary you with long descriptions of my recovery from the wounds inflicted on me by a German soldier throwing a British grenade at a British Grenadier in an Italian wood. Suffice it to say that at a Field Dressing Station they operated on me to remove lots of shrapnel and stitched up all my flesh wounds, and then they sent me to a hospital at Caserta, where I seemed to be mending nicely. Suddenly, however, I became very ill with trouble in one lung. It seemed that a tiny bit of something, clothing perhaps, had been blown into that lung and caused an abscess, and now I was flown down to hospital in Naples (the same one where I'd had jaundice eight months before).

Here things worsened, as I now had something called a cerebral embolus, a nasty business that made me – before I lost consciousness – feel sure that I was going mad. When I came to, I had been put in a single-bed side-room. Myrle's photograph was on the table beside me. I turned it back to front, saying, 'I shan't see her again.' However, this dramatic forecast turned out to be wrong. For thanks to that new wonder drug, penicillin, I gradually got better, well enough to be sent home in a hospital ship and then to hospital in Liverpool.

Eighty-eight Shell

The hair moves on the heads of dead men
In a little wind that is bitter with cordite
And sweet with the smell of death. All three
Lie starfished on the headland of the meadow.
When the shell came howling in through the hedge
One had his mouth full of chocolate, and
One had his mind full of girls, and one
Was watching a ladybird climbing his rifle.
The jaws are slack and the minds are blank
And eyeballs question the summer sky.
The rifle's crumpled. And what became
Of the ladybird, God alone knows.

1946

Chapter 4

A Home of Our Own

20 November
Mobbs' dispersal sale. Bought two cows and various oddments. Missed by bull.

When, some days later, the ward doors opened to admit visitors – wives, sweethearts, parents – one of those visitors was my own wife. Myrle told me later that she was frightened she wouldn't recognize me in the long line of beds containing sick men, many amputees among them. I must have looked very different to her from that day on the platform at Windsor Station. My weight had dropped from twelve stone to eight, and I had to lift one arm with the other in order to wave fondly at her. But seeing her again was, of course, the greatest of tonics and I began to get better.

A final irony was that on her second long journey by rail up to Liverpool to see me, she walked into the ward and there was my bed, empty. They had suddenly sent me to a convalescent home near Weston-super-Mare, and neither had been able to contact the other. She was now faced with a return journey with no return ticket and, what was worse, not enough money to pay her fare. With admirable aplomb she managed to find a seat in a compartment in which there was a number of officers who had decided to play poker to while away the long trip and kindly asked her, could she play? Would she like to? She could and she would and she won enough off them to do away with her worries about money.

From the convalescent home, I went to the only place I then thought of as home – the house where I'd been born. For the greatest part of two years Myrle and I lived with my parents, and my return to health is best judged by the fact that in October 1945 Myrle gave birth to a daughter, Juliet.

At around the same time I was invalided out of the army and my thoughts turned to farming again, the thing I'd always wanted to do. So back to the Wylye Valley went Myrle and I and the baby, accompanied by Anna, the first jointly owned dog we'd had.

Anna was a black and tan smooth-haired dachshund

and, when we had first collected her as a puppy, we feared she might be deaf, for she paid no attention to what we said to her. We learned there are dogs and there are dachshunds, strong-minded individuals who prefer to have things their own way always.

We lived in a tiny old house called Tudor Cottage, where the only bath was a tin one taken in front of the fire, and the only sort of lavatory was an earth-closet in the garden. The contents of this I would bury in the field behind, and because I used a rabbiting-spade with a curved blade, that field, when finally we left, was a strange sight, its ordinary grassy green stippled with a great number of perfectly round very dark green dots.

Tytherington Farm seemed suddenly to have jumped forwards into the twentieth century, you might say. The horses were almost all gone, machinery ruled, the downs were a sea of corn. Only Tom and Henry and Billy and the rest were just as I had remembered. Like the bombers we had then watched flying to Bristol, the war had passed over their heads and left them quite untouched.

I wasn't really much good on the farm, I wasn't yet

strong enough, but I still wanted to become a farmer, that was my long-held ambition. So the next move was to leave Myrle and the baby with Mother and Father, and go back to school, to an agricultural course, in fact, set up in a Wiltshire manor house for ex-servicemen.

I shared a bedroom with three other men. There was Tommy, who was not long out of hospital where they'd been treating him for what people in Father's war called 'shellshock'. There was Pat, the eldest of us, urbane and kindly, who knelt by his bed each night to say his prayers. There was Sandy, who on most nights was not there to see this, for he had acquired a local light-of-love with whom he passed his evenings. 'Shredded Wheat' he called her, and he always carried a mackintosh on these forays to lay her upon and save her from the damp. And there was me, only remarkable for the large cage that I kept in the bedroom, containing some hamsters. Unfortunately these in due course escaped and Lackham House (which is nowadays a very reputable agricultural college) suffered a hamster infestation, as the creatures colonized it and bred at speed. The German prisoners-of-war who were doing the cooking pursued them through the kitchens, brandishing soup-ladles.

Our course turned out to be a great deal shorter than planned because the winter of 1947 froze everything solid and we were all sent home for many weeks. But at the end everyone, dullards and laggards alike, was given a certificate, and we all set out to look for work in the agricultural industry, as cowmen or stockmen of some sort, perhaps as farm managers. Some, a very few, Pat for one, actually bought or rented a farm and began in business on their own account.

As for me, the family business came to my rescue. In the early years of the last century Grandfather, Charles King-Smith, had moved from a paper mill in Devon to take over one in a village called Bitton, in Gloucestershire, midway between Bristol and Bath. All paper mills need plentiful supplies of water, and the Golden Valley Paper Mills stood beside and fed off a tributary of the River Avon called the Boyd Brook, which ran slowly down the Golden Valley. The mill (oddly sometimes singular, sometimes plural) was a fairly small one, specializing in the making of high-quality paper, from rags rather than from wood-pulp, and it was very much a family firm.

After the Great War, Grampy K-S was joined by my father and by his next brother down, my Uncle Joe, who had been a prisoner of the Germans. He was really named Philip, but apparently as a boy he had had a favourite cat called Joe, who somehow lent him its name. Possibly they exchanged and the cat became Philip. I don't know.

Twenty or so years later, grandfather, father and uncle were joined at the mill by my brother, Tony, my cousin Beresford, and my Uncle Terence. There would, I suppose, have been space for me but by then I was set upon farming.

(What chaos I would have caused in the business had I had anything to do with its accounts!)

Golden Valley Paper Mills had done well during the war, and Father, with the agreement of Grampy K-S and Uncle Joe, decided that the firm would buy a small farm and there install me as manager, ostensibly to supply the mill canteen with milk and eggs. So off I went with my little diploma tucked underneath my arm, to look for a place of my own.

Hindsight makes Clever Dicks of us all, and it's easy for me now to see the long string of mistaken judgements that threaded through my farming life. Hastily and inadequately educated in the science and business of agriculture, after a spasmodic practical training on a huge downland chalk farm with no milking herd, I then, with no further experience, settled hastily upon a much too small dairy farm in poor order (heavy soil, no drainage, low fertility, good percentage of useless woodland). It was called Woodlands Farm (logical really, because seven or eight of its fifty acres were, indeed, covered in trees) on the edge of a village with the unromantic name of Coalpit Heath (again logical, for there had been open-cast mining there).

But at last we had a home of our own, our first proper home and now at last we were to be farmers.

I shall never forget the day of the dispersal sale at Woodlands Farm, when the previous farmer was moving out. The last lot on offer to the crowd of bidders was the bull. Six feet away, the Shorthorn bull stared fixedly at me with hot eyes. I don't remember thinking much about the length of his horns. But they did look sharp. He was blowing hard, and he shuffled his forefeet in the straw of the ring, like a boxer. Then he put his head down.

Up to this point it had been an unremarkable farm dispersal sale. They had dealt with the machinery and the implements, and all the usual job-lots – old tins of paint or grease, bottles of medicine for stock, coils of rusty barbed wire – for which there was always someone to bid half-a-crown or five shillings. There had been a few crates of ancient hens and a couple of fowl-houses. They had sold the young stock, and then the sixteen dairy cows, of which I had bought two, paying the top price and wearing a carefully contrived expression to show the assembled company that there wasn't much about a good milker that I didn't know. And then Lot Eighty-seven was called.

'Now then, gentlemen,' said the auctioneer in a voice rich with promise from his perch upon a four-wheeled wagon beside the rough circular sale-ring out in the yard. 'Now then! Last lot of the day, and worth waiting for as you will soon see.' He paused and looked up towards the open door of the cowshed. 'Bring him out, please.'

Heads turned as a confused noise arose from inside, of snorting and shouting and a low roaring.

'Lot Eighty-seven,' went on the auctioneer. 'Two-year-old light roan Dairy Shorthorn bull – come on, please, bring him along.' And at that moment there appeared in the doorway the son of the outgoing farmer, and the bull. It was not quite clear who was bringing whom along. Young Mobbs had hold of the bull-pole certainly, had the bull's head well up by the pressure of the pole on the nose-ring, but there was a certain air of desperation about him.

For a moment the bull stopped dead, bemused by the sudden sunlight and the crowd of people before him, and then three things happened. Young Mobbs lowered the tip of the pole, trying to drag the animal on into the ring. The bull, disregarding the pain in his nose, set his feet and pulled him back. And then a helpful bystander raised his stick, and with a loud cry of 'Get on, yer girt hummock!' brought it down upon the broad back of Lot Eighty-seven.

Five seconds later, the bull stood in the centre of the sale-ring, and as he swung his head from side to side, everyone could see the snap-link of the bull-pole dangling from his nose, while at the cowshed door young Mobbs gawped helplessly at the broken-off staff.

For the whole of that morning I had been in a dream, an understandably selfish dream. For me, this was no ordinary sale. Old Mobbs was going out and I was coming in. Things that I had bought: pig troughs, poultry fountains, pitchforks, fencing stakes, rolls of wire netting, would remain here, be used here. Lot Seventy (Buttercup) and Lot Seventy-one (Barbara) would stay and be milked in that cowshed, my cowshed. Dreamily I had stood among the press of local farmers around that makeshift ring of straw bales with a token fence of some old posts and a couple of strands of plain wire. Now suddenly there was an eruption of noise and movement.

Round the ring went the bull like a circus performer. Old Mobbs was standing with his hand resting on top of a fence-post as he watched his cattle sold, and one of those short horns sliced the meat off his thumb as neatly as a butcher's knife. Warning shouts drowned old Mobbs' cry of pain as the crowd melted away, into the cowshed, on to the wagon bed, behind walls, into sheds and loose-boxes. Old men, fat men, even lame men leaped for safety with the speed and agility of gazelles. Only the dreamer remained.

By chance, I was standing at a point nearest to the open orchard gateway. Out in the orchard the sold cows grazed happily, only the red-numbered labels glued on each between pin-bone and hook-bone showing this to be an unusual day. When, after several more circuits, the bull stopped and focused upon them, only I, frozen now into the inertia of nightmare, stood between. He put his head down.

Man can fly. I did. As the wire burst and the posts

cracked and the straw bales exploded like so much Weetabix, I flew, overcoat, boots and all, striking with my shoulder the closing-post of the orchard gate and snapping it off like a carrot. Inches behind came the thunder and wind of the bull's passing, and then he was gone, out into the herd, and away they all went in a mad gallop among the apple trees. I picked myself up, and then I heard my father's voice as he emerged from the nearby loose-box.

'Damn brave of the boy, Fred,' he said to a farmer of long acquaintance. 'He tried to stop him.'

'Stop un?' said Fred. 'He never. He were trying to bloody miss un.'

The 'boy' at that time was twenty-five. It was now three years since that hand-grenade had blown me sky-high in that dark Apennine wood. At last I was fit again, fit to fly for my life. We looked about for the bovine bomb that had just gone off, and saw him being shepherded back into the cowshed, safely hedged about with puffing blowing cows. Nobody, it seemed, was keen to buy him, and when I went to see him later they had made a belt-and-braces job of his security. Round his thick neck was a heavy plaited chain, and a short rope led from his ring to a stanchion at the back of the standing. As bulls do, he screwed his head round slowly and rolled one eye at me. I'll be happier when you're gone, you rascal you, I thought.

A week later the lorry came to take him to the knacker's. We tied a length of rope through his ring, led it right up the shed, and through a pulley at the far end of the lorry bed. Helpers unchained him, and carefully I took the strain and winched him up. He went in like a lamb.

'Fuss about nothing,' said the lorry driver as we locked up the tail-gate. 'Wouldn't hurt a fly. I knows a bad bull when I sees one. Thissun won't give no trouble.'

Later, the news filtered back. The smells, the sights, and the sounds of the abattoir were by no means to the liking of old Mobbs' bull, and he had come out of the lorry like a tornado. Around the slaughterhouse he went, smashing anything in his path and refusing all attempts to pen him. I don't know what the proprietors of chinashops do, but these slaughtermen kept a high-powered rifle for such a contingency as this, and they called up their marksman. So the Shorthorn bull perished, but not at the first shot. In the general confusion the rifleman must have loosed off a little carelessly. The bull kept galloping, but above the rumble of his hoofs was heard a cry of pain as an onlooker fell with a bullet in his shoulder.

It was Gladwyn who told me the final twist in the tale of old Mobbs' bull. Gladwyn was a Welshman from the Valleys, a year or so younger than me, who had worked for the Mobbs family and stayed on to work for us, for fifteen years as it turned out. We were mucking out the pen where the late beast had lived in semi-darkness. It was in a section – two stalls' worth – of the old stables, lit by a small window only. No ray of sunlight had ever entered. In the gloom at the far end, another of my purchases, Bob the one-eyed carthorse, stamped and ground his teeth.

I said, 'You can't wonder that that poor devil went wild on getting out of this dim poky hole. Did he ever see the light of day?'

'Oh, we used to take him outside for service,' said Gladwyn. 'Mind you,' he said, 'it would have been awkward with the roof being a bit low, but they'd sooner have brought the cow in here.'

'Why?'

'More discreet, see.'

'Discreet?'

Gladwyn had a sudden high shrieking laugh, often ending in copious weeping if the joke was funny enough. He whinnied loudly now, and Bob started against his head-rope.

'Mr Mobbs thought it was rude,' said Gladwyn, and he began to cry. When at last I got the facts from him, between snorts and snuffles and much mopping of the eyes, they were these.

Whenever a cow or heifer in the Mobbs' herd had come on bulling, an unvarying routine took place at Woodlands Farm. First, old Mobbs would order young Mobbs, then rising eighteen, into the house, and would ensure that Mrs Mobbs and Miss Mobbs were also within. All the curtains would be drawn. Only then would old Mobbs bring the cow down from the cowshed on a halter, while with the bull-pole Gladwyn fetched out the bull from the stables, and stood by during the short ceremony.

Old Mobbs' eyes, Gladwyn assured me tearfully, flicked anxiously from window to window the while. Then the two beasts would be put away, old Mobbs would go to the back door and order the curtains to be opened, and the family would continue their polite way of life, unsullied by the facts of it. When they left Woodlands Farm, the Mobbs's went market-gardening. Vegetables, after all, are so much more circumspect.

Chapter 5

WOODLANDS FARM

Sunday 29 February
3rd in Lent.
Buttercup calved, bull calf. Myrle had baby
girl 10.50 a.m. (7 lb). Both well.

In fact, we did not move into the farmhouse until early in 1948, Myrle and I and the baby Juliet and our three dogs, Anna the dachshund, her son Jonah (he was to become a champion) and my terrier Susie, whom I had bought as a puppy from Jack the horseman at Tytherington Farm (the price was two packets of Woodbines). Our move was only just in time, for Myrle was heavily pregnant and the first of my thick stack of farm diaries carried the above announcement for Leap Year's Day in 1948.

The previous afternoon we had been to the cinema in Bristol. The fact that Myrle was thirty-nine weeks pregnant was not going to interfere with one of our routine pleasures. *Mine Own Executioner* the film was called, and about halfway through the pains began.

'What d'you think happened just now?' Myrle said, after we had fought our apologetic way along the row to the gangway.

'What?'

'A man pinched my bottom.'

'It's very dark in here.'

By chance we had left the car in what looked like a public car park but must, in fact, have belonged to some firm or business premises. As I approached it, supporting the mother-to-be, I could see that its tall iron spear-pointed gates were shut. There was a latch but it was on the inside and I couldn't reach it through the bars. The high stone walls on either side were topped with bits of broken bottles. Inside, passport to home and warmth and safety and doctors and midwives, stood the car. I began to climb the gates. By the time we reached Woodlands Farm the pains had stopped.

By 5 o'clock on Sunday morning, it was plain that this baby was in no mood to wait for March the first, when the monthly nurse was booked to arrive, and so I was on my way to fetch the local midwife. On arrival she was greeted by the three dogs, Anna, Jonah and Susie. She drew up her skirts in distaste. 'We shall want them shut away,' said the midwife, and, on entering the bedroom, 'We shall need newspapers, plenty of newspapers. And boiling water.'

Then, as I still don't, I never saw any use for the boiling water, but the armfuls of newspapers that I carried upstairs were laid everywhere – on the bed, under the bed, all over the floor, even upon chairs and tables. By the time the doctor arrived the place was a sea of newsprint. Myrle was being extremely stoical, only seeming every now and then to give voice to a curious whining sound. Ventriloquially, it came not from the bed but from beneath it.

Suddenly the midwife dropped heavily to her knees, and splaying herself out like a giraffe at a waterhole (for the bed was very low) peered beneath it.

'There's a dog here!' she cried.

All dachshunds are stubborn and Anna was especially so. Our bed – we still sleep in it – is a large one. The baby that was about to arrive would be of the third generation, following myself and my mother, to have been both conceived and born upon it. The space beneath it was too cramped for anyone to get hold of Anna, and she was deaf to threats or blandishments. So she was present at the birth.

Later in the day, Father arrived to view the new (red-haired) baby girl. Never the most tactful of men, he excelled himself on this occasion. 'Wrong sex again, eh,

Myrle?' he said, and earned himself an earful from his furious daughter-in-law.

The next morning, Sister Cartwright duly arrived, a round, comfortable, smiling person. Everything looked good at Woodlands Farm. Mother and child had had a restful night. Gladwyn and I had milked the cows (I'd bought about ten by then. Fancy! Nowadays one man milks a hundred or more). The horse, Bob, and Molly, first of the pigs, had been fed. The dogs lay happily about in a bedroom free of newspapers and the kettle was being used for the understandable purpose of making tea. What was there for a newly arrived highly qualified monthly nurse to do? Hardly had she taken off her sensible belted grey tweed overcoat than Gladwyn's head came round the kitchen door.

'The pullets!' he cried in ringing tones.

'What? Oh Lor', what with having to fetch Sister and one thing and another I forgot to feed them.'

'You needn't bother now, see,' said Gladwyn.

A couple of weeks before I had bought a dozen fine Light Sussex pullets on the point of lay. They were housed, out in the orchard, in a home-made ex-Mobbs run that could be moved about over the grass. It was quite a stout contraption with a roof over it, and because it had a floor of chicken wire I had no fears for the safety of the birds.

What I had not bargained for was that the five-centimetre mesh of the floor netting would admit part of a long nose. The fox had scratched and scrabbled away to make a tunnel under the run, and had worked his way beneath the birds. Carry them away he could not, but he had forced his muzzle through the wire time and time again, and pulled and bitten at anything that came within his reach, a wing-tip, a leg, a throat, as the wretches blundered about in the moonlight. Nine of the twelve lay sprawled and dead, of loss of blood or limb, or of shock.

'Look at these three, boyo,' said Gladwyn, softly. 'Poor buggers.' The unhappy survivors squatted with outstretched wings, their beaks wide, the nictitating membranes agitating over their reproachful eyes. In their breasts, part plucked by the urgent fox, there were gaping holes.

'I'll hit 'em out, shall I?' said Gladwyn.

'Yes. No, wait a minute.'

We carried them to the kitchen, for the inspection of professional eyes.

'What d'you think, Carty? Any chance of saving them?'

'Easy as wink, dear. Get some newspaper on the table here. And put the kettle on.'

And out of her little black bag came needle and surgical thread and dressings and antiseptic.

Monday 1 March. St David
Carty arrived, sewed up three pullets.
Fox had the other nine. To Chipping Sodbury to register Betsy's birth.

If the Mad Hatter and the March Hare had put their heads together and planned the stocking of Woodlands Farm, the results could hardly have been more higgledy-piggledy than those that I achieved all by myself. It was so when we were children and had graduated from our collections of toy farm animals to actual livestock, in fact to breeding budgerigars.

Myrle had practised colour-breeding, green or cobalt or sky-blue birds confined to their separate compartments or 'flights', each pair creating budgies in their own image. Male and female created they them, and all was order and neatness, Virgo style. But in Aries' aviary, I mated everybody happily to everybody else to produce offspring of unconventional shades, rather as a child indiscriminately mixes various coloured sticks of plasticine and ends up with a muddy mess. Green being dominant, my flock became a collection of greenish birds with bits of blue about them, not to be compared with those Virgoan budgies. Unable to match the competition, I went in for foreign finches.

But at Woodlands Farm I had the field, or rather the cowshed, to myself. I began to acquire a body of cattle that would have made Fred Karno's Army look uniform. Anyone with any sense would have decided upon a breed, and laid out every penny to fill the twenty-four standings with down-calving or freshly-calved heifers, or at the oldest, second calvers; would have bought good quality commercial beasts from carefully selected dispersal sales, or through a reputable dealer; would have concentrated every effort and all available money towards getting back a decent monthly milk cheque just as soon as possible. Not me.

You must believe (I must believe, my diary tells me) that by 10 March 1948, having had possession for four months, I had the apt number of thirteen cows in milk. They were of all ages and sizes, and bore as little resemblance to each other as was bovinely possible.

True, a number of them were Shorthorns of one type or another (pretty colours, you see, all different, not like boring old Friesians), some being first calvers bought from Tytherington for old times' sake. But in addition there were a couple of Ayrshires with horns like hat-racks, a blue-grey beast, the second cousin of a Jersey, and a very small short-legged animal of unknown origin that had been someone's house-cow, kept in his garage. I fell for her because of her cute size and pretty mottled markings; she gave as much milk as a goat.

Take Auntie. She was a good example of my technique. I bought her from Bill Tanner whom I'd known since I played around his farmyard as a small boy. Thinking about it, Auntie was probably there then, she was so old. A smallish Ayrshire with a kind sad face and lovely long white eyelashes, her overgrown hoofs curled like pairs of Turkish sandals, her back dipped like a fairground swing-boat, and her drooping hairy bag, its four great teats like bananas, was just what a dairy cow's udder shouldn't be. But she was so gentle and quiet (not having the energy to be otherwise), and so cheap, a real bargain. The bargain of course was Bill's, since I paid him much more than he'd have got from the knacker. Before the year was out, that's where poor Auntie went, dry, barren and bony.

I fancied myself as a good striker of a deal. Buy or sell, I must have been everybody's sucker.

Look what my thirteen cows were producing.

Wednesday 10 Monday
New Moon.
Sent 30 gallons away.

Surely I didn't record that out of pride? Probably it was the first time we'd reached such a figure. Of course I never could see, still can't sometimes, that if you want a pair of decent shoes you have to pay good money for them. I prowled around the local sales and markets till I'd filled the shed with mongrel mediocrities. Not that they seemed so at the time. Each, I thought, was in some way remarkable. They all had carefully chosen names, they were well cared for and generously fed, their mating and their calvings properly conducted, their slightest ailment promptly treated. Sometimes the vet seemed practically to live upon the place, so solicitous was I of the health of my herd. In large measure, they were pets. Too few cows giving too little milk – not the ideal start to dairy farming.

We compounded this first basic shortcoming because of this pet-loving mentality – the miscellaneous collection of painted lead animals proudly set out upon the nursery floor – and filled every spare space at Woodlands Farm with one or another bird or beast. On farms, we knew, you could keep all kinds of creatures. We kept them.

Leaving aside the household animals – three dogs soon to be many, two cats soon to be a legion, and counted in with them the rabbits, the guinea-pigs, the mice, the budgerigars (all these we still had), the tortoises set to race on the lawn (first to fall in the flower-bed wins) – we wanted to and did keep every kind of living thing that took our fancy. They'll earn their keep, we thought, producing eggs or meat or saleable young. They mustn't just be passengers.

We never in fact kept sheep, because a public footpath ran through the middle of the farm and we feared worrying from local dogs, but instead we bought goats, and tethered them all over the shop. They were to provide milk for puppy-rearing. Though they were as varied in their origins as the cows and, proportionately, as unproductive, there was hardly one that hadn't been an absolute bargain. And there are few sights so attractive as that of newborn kids skipping around.

We didn't have horses, if you don't count Bob and we didn't count him for long. As a colt (a very long time ago), he had put one eye out in a thorn hedge and this affected his idea of a straight line, whereas the Ferguson tractor was young and didn't move diagonally or grind its teeth. Bob was given one last good gallop among the blackberry bushes in the woods and then sent to Doyle the knacker who, to our horror, turned up later that day.

He carried two large still-warm lumps of meat.

'Oi thought ye moight loike a bit for the dogs.'

I can't think why we didn't have any donkeys. Delightful creatures, I feel sure we should have made some excuse for keeping them.

But we kept a great variety of poultry. Chickens – growers, layers, table birds, of a host of different varieties, gamebirds both full-size and bantam; pheasants, guinea-fowl, geese, ducks; again, why no turkeys?

Last of all there were the pigs, supposedly second only to the cows as a commercial enterprise, but for my money – which is what they gobbled up – far superior in native intelligence, good common sense, and beauty of form and feature.

And all these mooing, grunting, bleating, squawking, quacking things were of surpassing interest to us, characters, with names and personalities.

There was always something fascinating going on. But did they pay their way, I hear you ask. Sorry?

This motley conglomeration of creatures that you seem to have surrounded yourself with – were they commercially viable?

Well, we got a lot of fun out of –

Surely you kept proper accounts?

Yes, of course. After a fashion.

Well, did they show a profit?

Oh dear.

The play had only just begun, the curtain hardly risen, but, had we known it, the fateful figure of that bank manager already stood in the darkness of the wings, awaiting his entry at the end of the second act.

Chapter 6

Cows

Sunday 21 November
26th after Trinity.
My day off, but Gladwyn to see his father
in hospital so I worked.

There's always something to do on a farm every hour of daylight, every day of the year. On a small place like Woodlands Farm, so much, with proper planning, could have been done single-handed. At most it was man-and-a-boy stuff. Yet there we were, Gladwyn and I, solemnly sharing the milking, the care of stock, the cultivations, the field work. Mind you, I couldn't have done without him when it came to the mysteries of the internal-combustion engine, which to me have always been

65

Eleusinian. All I knew, and know, is how to satisfy the liquid needs of tractor or car.

But generally the labour of the farm was shared. Gladwyn and I milked the cows on alternate days, the other seeing to the feeding of the remaining animals. We took alternate Saturday afternoons and Sundays off, and every year, scrupulously, one would have Christmas Day off, one Boxing Day. As for holidays we took, in turn, two weeks holiday each in the summer time between haymaking and harvest.

By 1953 Myrle and I had three children – the two girls (by that date aged eight and five) and Giles, who had appeared, presumably much to Father's approval ('Right sex at last, eh?'). For our holidays the five of us went – as always – to West Wales, to Tenby in Pembrokeshire.

Some time in the 1890s a great-great-uncle had been there and reported that it was a very pleasant place, so all members of the family then went there every year for the next sixty or seventy years.

Indeed it was on the Royal Victoria Pier at Tenby in Pembrokeshire that my father first saw my mother.

It was the summer of 1920, and she was recently eighteen years old. He, nearing twenty-six and with a DSO and an MC to show for his service in the Great War, was still on crutches after having being badly wounded.

Somehow he found out where this pretty girl was staying and that she was confined to her room with a cold, and he positioned himself down on the sands of the South Beach. By sheer luck, I suppose, Mother appeared at the window of a house high above, and Father, supporting himself on one crutch, drew with the toe of the other in large capital letters on the Tenby sands:

GET WELL SOON.

Even now the town exerts a magnetic pull.

Each day at Woodlands Farm started, of course, with morning milking. Sometimes, especially in summer, it was pleasant work, but sometimes it was hell.

Try this scenario:

5.45 a.m.: Alarm goes. Stumble out of bed, aware in one horrid instant that I've only had three or four hours' sleep. Whatever it was we drank last night with whichever friends, my head is splitting. Dress in the very cold dark, feeling heroic, so as not to wake Myrle. Tiptoe out and press switch of landing light. Nothing. Damn, bulb gone. Not so, no other lights work. Power failure. Blast. No tea. Open back door to let dogs out, whereupon four cats, the east wind, and a barrowload of snow come in.

6.00 a.m.: Begin trying to start tractor – to run milking-machine engine by belt and pulley.

6.45 am.: Gladwyn arrives and starts tractor.

7.00 a.m.: Start milking (just light enough to see what I'm doing) while Gladwyn sets about unthawing various taps, cows' water-bowls, etc.

During milking, these diversions occur: belt keeps slipping off pulley, therefore suctionless units fall off cows, who promptly trample them. Power comes on again. Disconnect tractor. Switch on milking-machine engine. Turn on all lights. Breathe sigh of relief. Power goes off again, engine stops, units fall off, lights go out. Reconnect tractor. Thompson, the one (giant) Friesian, stands on my toes. I thump her. She kicks me on the shin. Bout of lunatic laughter from passing Gladwyn. Hard to believe, but headache is worsening, eclipsing pain in toes and leg. Carry full small churns to dairy (twenty-four mincing paces on icy surface). Slip, fall down, top comes off one churn, four gallons of milk gush out over concrete, half a dozen more cats appear from nowhere. Belt slips off again, units fall off again. Feel sick.

Reach Midnight, notorious kicker, normally needs her hocks tying with rope. Can't be bothered, get my shoulder well under her and lean in hard, hoping for best. Worst happens. With one tremendous wallop she comprehensively strips the machine bucket – air-line, milk-pipe, pulsator, teat-cups – flying in all directions, while I finish on my backside in urine-filled dung-channel.

At last, the final cow, good gentle Martha. Remove the units from her udder, give her a pat, and as I pass behind her she shits and coughs simultaneously, spraying me from chin to crutch. As I approach the dairy I can see the milk rushing down the drain from the overflowing churn.

A jolly little voice cries, 'Mummy says breakfast in ten minutes!'

'I don't want any breakfast.'

A wet snowball hits me in the back of the neck.

Of all the cows I kept, there are bound to be some that I shan't forget, the 'characters'. Once they had established themselves, they remained comfortingly predictable. When Virgil says that 'Woman is always fickle and changing', you can tell straight away that he was never inside a cowshed. I look back now on the females in mine and know that they were constant.

You knew that Buttercup, the master cow, was an eminently sensible individual who under no circumstances would commit any anti-social act. A big-boned, red-and-white animal with short curled horns and big flat feet, she led the herd through every gateway. She was universally deferred to on account of her majestic, ponderous gentleness.

Cissie, you knew, could be guaranteed to behave as foolishly as possible on all occasions. She would leap in terror at the rustle of a mouse. To make a pun, she was the butt of every other cow. At the sight of the vet, even for the humblest of injections, she would roar with fright, her bowels turned instantly to water. Every gate was a place of terror to her, for those in front hooked her as she tried to pass and those behind did too as she then held back. To go through last would have been sensible, but you could tell by her rolling eye that her conviction was that then Gladwyn or I would beat her to death with our sticks, or the dogs would leap up (quite a long way for most of them) and tear out her throat.

I bought a small rusty-black sharp-horned beast of Kerry blood, and toyed therefore with the notion of giving her some Irish name like Siobhan, but she named herself the first time I milked her. Some cows let fly when you put the teat-cups on them, some while they are being milked, some when you remove the clusters. Kicker did all three. But unlike most kicking cows, who object to the act of milking for reasons of innate nervousness or previous ill-usage or sore teats, Kicker, like a professional footballer, practised the art for its own sake, so that to pass between her and her neighbour was not something to be done absent-mindedly. Worse, like a mule she could kick through an arc of 180 degrees, and to stand or walk too close behind her was to invite trouble; immediate, lightning-swift, deadly accurate. You could rely on Kicker.

You could rely on Thompson for unshakeable placidity. A huge pedigree British Friesian, bought as a third calver, she was the first of that breed to enter my cowshed. Bred on the chalk, she had bone like a rhinoceros, a bag like a barrage balloon, and feet that made old Buttercup's seem almost dainty. All her actions were carried out with monumental slowness, her walk, the business of getting up or lying down, the turn of her head, even the movement of her jaw when chewing the cud. Her reactions were as sluggish. If Thompson stood (accidentally: she hadn't an ounce of vice in her) on your foot, no amount of angry swearing or agonized yelling or frantic thumping of her massive sides would release you until the snail-pace message reached her brain to say that something was amiss.

You could depend on Polly for a laugh, sometimes a wry one. Like all good comedians there was a look about her that made you smile, without a moo spoken. Part of the reason for this was that she was a pure-bred Ayrshire, a breed with a big spread of horn, but had been dehorned – polled – as a calf, hence her name. In those times this made her appear quaint. She also had an extremely long giraffe-neck and a face that seemed more mobile than the rest, and therefore more comical. People smiled when they looked at Polly and seemed half to expect in return a nod of recognition or a wink of complicity, so knowing did she look.

If she had spoken, it would have been about food, for her other hallmark was an insatiable appetite. It was Polly who always finished her cake or hay before anyone else and was then busy contorting that long neck to steal her neighbour's. It was Polly you kept the most careful eye on if the herd was turned out on to something a bit lush, for she'd be the first to be blown. It was Polly who found gaps in hedges, made holes in fences, and even, I sometimes thought, lifted the latches of gates to get at the grass that was greener on the other side.

One night she nearly ate herself to death.

Since I'd turned part of the cowshed into a fodder store, we always kept the connecting door closed in case a cow should get loose overnight. Because Polly had no horns, a chain would not hold her, and she always wore a leather collar, buckled as tight as was possible. On this particular night, three mischances coincided. Her collar was slack, the door had been left ajar, and in the store were a number of bags of raw linseed, the harvest of one of my experiments with growing esoteric crops.

In the morning I could hear the groans before I was halfway up the yard, and ran, and there was her stall empty. For once there was nothing to laugh at about Polly. She lay like a foundered whale in a shallow sea of linseed, gorged with the oily stuff, her belly blown out to twice its normal size so that the giraffe-neck seemed unnaturally thin. Her ears drooped, making the bony boss of her poll stand up like a little bowler hat. Pathos and comedy were joined, as though Stan Laurel's head was stuck on Oliver Hardy's body.

God knows how much of the linseed she had eaten. All one could say with certainty was that it couldn't have happened to a greedier cow. I ran to phone the vet.

For three days and nights she lay there, covered in sacking to keep her warm, turned from one side to the other with ropes and enormous effort, emitting rivers of dung rich enough to grow Jack's beanstalk. A lesser beast would have died, but not Polly. The vet and Gladwyn and I may have contributed something to her recovery, but what got her to her feet again was undoubtedly the thought of the next square meal.

Finally, for sheer meanness, you could rely on Midnight.

Of all the many purchases I made, Midnight's was the most impulsive. A local farmer was selling up, it was a lovely day, there was nothing that absolutely had to be done for an hour or so.

'Come on,' I said to Gladwyn. 'We'll just pop over and have a look.'

I hadn't thought seriously of buying anything, hadn't

been round the cattle before, hadn't even set eyes on the magnificent wild animal that suddenly ran into the ring. In a flash the scene changed for me, from Gloucestershire to Granada. There was sand in the ring, not straw, and round it not bales but the *barrera*. Behind that sat the *aficionados*, farmers and dealers no longer, and stared down with eyes narrowed against the blazing Spanish sun.

The cow (it was almost a shock to see the evidence of its sex) stood there, the blackest cow you ever did see, coal black, raven black, black as midnight, and I suddenly said to Gladwyn, 'What d'you think of that one?'

'Not a lot.'

'Nice tackle,' I said. 'There's some milk there.' And indeed she had a well-hung udder, deep, square, flat-soled, the good-sized teats well placed.

'Got a funny look in her eye, boyo,' said Gladwyn.

The cow shook her small sharp horns at the drover who was moving her round the ring.

'And I wouldn't like one of those antlers up my arse.'

'I shan't go above fifty,' I said. They were making a good bit more than that. She'd be a snip at fifty, I thought.

Funnily enough nobody seemed much to want her.

'I bought a cow up at Goose Green,' I said to Myrle when we got home.

'What sort of a cow?'

'Well, no particular sort. She's black. Second calver. Rather a beautiful beast.'

'How much?'

'Forty pounds.'

'Three-quartered is she, or three-legged, or what?'

'No. Just a bargain'.

But I got more than I'd bargained for.

The haulier brought Midnight in time for the afternoon milking, and what a milking that was. At the first touch of the first cup on the first teat she put on a performance that relegated Kicker to the fourth division. It wasn't just the kicking, explosively violent, a burst of heavy machine-gun fire instead of Kicker's little pistol shots, a fusillade that stripped the machinery into its component parts and left Gladwyn and me battered and bruised and breathless. It was the sheer ferocity that accompanied the act, as she leaped and pranced and bucketed, blaring and bawling at us with wide-open mouth, not in pain or fear but in red-hot anger. Her fierce eyes blazed, and only the neck-chain restrained her from her obvious wish to disembowel the pair of us with those twin daggers.

So it was at every milking. Even with her hind legs tied and a vice-like instrument called 'the bulldogs' in her nostrils, she still could contrive enough galvanic heaves to shake off the units, still bellow her hatred and fury.

Any theory I might have had that Midnight's black Satanic anger was directed solely against the milking-machine was dispelled a week later. It was Gladwyn's day off, and Myrle had walked out with me when I went to fetch the cows in. She stopped to pick some wild flowers from a bank, and I went over the hill.

When next I saw Myrle, she was on the other side of a fence, rather white about the face and very angry.

'That bloody Midnight!'

'Why, what happened?'

'The moment she saw me, she put her head down and started to paw up the ground, and then she gave a horrible kind of roar and came straight for me.'

'Good God, what did you do?'

'What d'you think? Got through this fence of course. She's mad.'

'Gladwyn did say she had a funny look in her eye.'

'You should listen to what Gladwyn says in future.'

'Yes. She'll have to go.'

They all did, in the end of course, one way or another, Midnight and Polly and Thompson and Kicker and Cissie and Buttercup the boss, and all the rest of them. A dairy cow's life is not often as long as it might be. The vet, the butcher, the knacker, they're all waiting, and seldom does anyone die in her bed. But the look of each and every one of them is clear in my mind.

One other bovine character who stands out in memories of Woodlands Farm was Ben-the-bull, so called to distinguish him from a friend called Ben. Ben-the-bull was an Aberdeen Angus just like those black beauties that had roamed the downs at Tytherington. Though you should never trust a bull, he was in fact very quiet and biddable. However, one never-to-be-forgotten day, Ben-the-bull escaped.

I had never been able to bring myself to run Ben out with the cows. Woodlands Farm was a very different matter from Tytherington, and it had a public footpath going right across it. Moreover, however quiet he seemed, bulls will be bulls, and I worried on the children's behalf. So customarily he lived quite happily out in the orchard on a length of running chain, and was brought into the yard for service (though we didn't pull any curtains).

On this occasion he had been for some reason tied up in the cowshed, with that same heavy metal that had once held Mobbs' bull. But, unlike Mobbs' bull, Ben had no horns, and when the cows had been milked and turned out he had decided to go walkabout. He had slipped his thick neck out, and, though all the doors of the cowshed had been left wide open, had decided for some good reason of his own upon a different means of exit. He set his brow against the wooden wall and pushed.

I know that this is what happened, because at that precise moment I chanced to come out into the yard, to see his head emerging through the cowshed wall, just as a circus dog jumps through a paper hoop. With a splintering crash his body followed, while pieces of stout timber and planking flew in all directions. He lumbered off into the nearest field, called the Railway Ground, which had a heavy green-fodder crop of oats and vetches, and stood there belly-deep in the stuff, a few yards inside the gate, a bovine Billy Bunter loose in an unguarded tuck-shop.

Before I could move, Gladwyn arrived back from his breakfast, cycling into the yard. Catching sight of Ben staring owlishly at him, he did not dismount but with wild cries of Welsh anger rode straight into the field as if to ram the great black barrel of a bull, and fell off.

Alarmed by the sudden and noisy appearance of this human torpedo, Ben started off up the hill at a ponderous gallop, smashing his way through the tangle of oats and vetches, while Gladwyn, cursing horribly, struggled through them in a vain attempt to cut him off.

I was laughing so much that I couldn't do anything, but managed to dash the tears from my eye in time to witness a wonderful scene. I only have to shut them to summon it up now.

Ben had reached the public footpath, and he turned to gallop along it, directly across my field of vision. And because the path ran along the crown of the farm, making a near horizon, the picture was in stark silhouette against the morning sky.

Fit and furious, and free now of the entangling crop, Gladwyn closed rapidly on the fat and flagging Ben. Halfway across he was near enough to grasp the tail of the bull and throw his weight against it, like the anchor man in a tug-of-war team. And by the time that a hedge cut them off from my sight, Ben was down to a trot.

Pulling myself together, I found the bull-pole and began to run across the paddock to find them, only to see, now walking towards me, the heaving blowing figure of a breathless Ben, meekly following a panting Gladwyn.

'D'you want me to put him on the pole?'

'Darw, boyo, the silly old bugger don't need no pole, see. He's run out of puff, silly old sod. Look here.' And I could see that Gladwyn had just one finger, the little one, hooked through Ben's nose-ring.

Ben's story has a happy ending. When I decided to dispense with him, I felt strongly that I would like him to go to a really good home. And suddenly I thought – Of course! Tytherington! That'd be the life for him.

So I wrote to my old master there, and he was perfectly agreeable, either for old times' sake, or, more probably, because I was asking too modest a price.

And for many years afterwards, I like to think, for he was only a youngster, the gleaming satiny black shape of

Ben-the-bull roamed the rolling downlands with his many-coloured heifers, and passed on to hundreds of sons and daughters his quiet and amiable ways.

Chapter 7

Pigs

Wednesday 27 May
Monty off his food. Vet to see.

As well as cow-keeping, we began pig-keeping. The poor old pig, linked always with gluttony, obesity and squalor. As greedy as ... as fat as ... as dirty as ... In fact, pigs are very like us. Their digestive systems are almost identical to ours, they are omnivorous as we are, and they very much enjoy their food, as we do. They are also intelligent, strong-willed, and of an independent nature, all gifts we admire in ourselves. We can hardly blame them for fatness and greed, since we have bred and fed them for just such qualities, licking our lips with an anticipation that is almost cannibal as we lean upon the wall of a sty and look down upon these creatures that so nearly resemble us.

As for being dirty (by which we mean not just muddy but incontinent), given half a chance there is no cleaner animal on the farm. Humans, once out of nappies, pride themselves on confining their excretions to a particular spot, as opposed to the random discharge of cattle or sheep or poultry; and they instruct the dogs and cats that share their houses to respect that privilege. But without any training the pig from an early age will use a lavatory only if he is given one.

As for intelligence, when next you get a chance, look closely into a pig's eye. The expression in the eye of a dog is trusting, of a cat supercilious, of a cow ruminative, of a sheep vacuous. But the look in the eye of a pig is, quite simply, knowing. Other beasts think, 'This human is looking at me.' The pig thinks, 'I am looking at this human.' There is all the difference in the world.

My pig-keeping could best be described as amateurish with flashes of professionalism. The pigs suffered more than the other livestock from my love of trying to do things on the cheap. For example, I fed my store pigs large amounts of swill, cooked swill that arrived weekly in great steaming drums, filled with waste food of every imaginable kind, including on two occasions whole boiled cats. These had presumably fallen into the vats from some overhead mousing walkway, and been cooked. The pigs chomped them up with gusto. They seemed to love swill. But they fattened rather slowly.

At Woodlands Farm we converted the old barn into a modest piggery, dividing the floor space with walls into a narrow feeding passage at the front, four roomy sties through the middle, and at the back a dung-passage running the whole length and divided by a system of doors so that each sty had its own latrine. Mucking out was a simple matter of shovelling, brushing, and hosing down the dung-passage, which forty pigs had meticulously used. The sties themselves would be spotless.

The conversion of the barn was a sensible enough idea: a good investment and well designed. The same could not be said of the housing that I provided for the sows to farrow outside. Most people would have invested in good strong weatherproof huts built for the purpose, with stout floors and farrowing rails, and skids and proper linkage for easy moving. Not I, I bought a job lot of old fowl houses. I removed the perches but left the nest-boxes on as an escape area for piglets at risk of being overlaid. I also took the wheels off and thus lowered the ancient structures to the ground, having just enough wit to realize that otherwise a 350-pound sow would go straight through the floor.

When we came to move the first of them to fresh ground, in a field aptly named the Wilderness, we hooked a chain on to it and pulled merrily away with the tractor. Whereupon the whole thing fell to pieces like a pack of cards. Later movings were nervous occasions, each hen-house tied up with rope like a giant parcel. Gladwyn and I would proceed with the utmost caution, one driving the Ferguson at snail's pace, the other monitoring progress with anxious shouts of 'Hold it! She's twisting!' or 'Steady! The floor's going!'

There was however one successful economy, the fencing of The Wood. This three-acre block of humps and hollows covered with a tangle of trees and undergrowth was useless for any other purpose. It would be ideal, I thought, to run pigs in. For shelter there were two good brick-built Nissen huts, in which the Home Guard had once stored their ammunition. There were many oak trees whose acorns in due season would be gratefully received. And there would be no need to ring the pigs, for they could root away to their hearts' content. True, there was no drinking water laid on, but that was easily solved – an old bath at the nearest point to the tap, and a length of hose. Why spend money on a proper field-tank and piping? No need even for feeding-troughs. Take a bag of pig-nuts and throw them on the ground.

The only problem was one of containment. The perimeter of The Wood was perhaps 600 yards, of which 100 were walled. So I should need 500 yards of pig-wire, a formidable outlay. And in practical terms, though the pigs would be unable to get through or over it, how could I be certain that they wouldn't squeeze under it? Somewhere, especially on such rough and steep ground, someone would find or force a way beneath the bottom strand, and the thought of three or four dozen pigs making their way to Bristol or Chipping Sodbury was nightmarish. Any fence must be pig proof or I should never sleep easy.

I went to the sawmills.

'Coffin boards,' said the sawyer. 'It's coffin boards you want.'

'Coffin boards?'

'Like these.'And he showed me a stack of them, long slices of elm an inch or so thick and six feet in length. 'Not good enough for the undertaker, these ones. Got a split or a shake or a knothole in them. Ideal for your job.'

'But they're only two foot high. Any pig'd get over them'.

'Ah, for the base to your fence, I do mean, young man. Set them well down flush to the ground with a stake driven against them either end, and then all you do want is a bit of wire on top of 'em.'

And that way it wouldn't need to be so high, I thought, so I bought not 500 but 250 yards of pig-wire and Gladwyn and I solemnly cut it all in half longwise

And then round The Wood we went with our stakes and our coffin boards and our foreshortened wire. And over the years hundreds of pigs lived there happily, and not one ever escaped.

This kind of success story was not the general rule. Take my dealings with dealers. Later, in the heyday of the Woodlands pigs when I was running ten sows with my own boar and producing at least a hundred and fifty weaners a year, there were plenty to fill the sties and a surplus to sell. But in the first days, when the only pig on the place was a large white gilt called Molly that I had bought from the farm attached to a local lunatic asylum, I had to buy 'slips' – eight- to ten-week-old youngsters, just off the sow. I knew the sort of pig I wanted to buy and I knew the sort of price I wanted to pay, and even now it amazes me how seldom the two coincided.

What a joy I must have been to Mr Hamper.

Mr Hamper was distinguishable from his larger pigs by virtue of wearing clothes and standing on his hind legs. Even then his face was so porcine that it was almost a surprise to see hands rather than trotters protruding from the sleeves of his ancient dust-coat. Above his several chins, thick lips that half-hid yellowish tusks were topped by a squashed nose whose nostrils pointed forward like the mouth of an aimed shotgun. His cheeks hung pendulous, his little eyes glinted, and he always wore, perhaps to conceal huge hairy ears, a woollen hat like a giant's tea-cosy.

Behind Mr Hamper's house was a yard flanked by a range of a dozen brick-built pigsties, in the nearest of which my trading with him always began, since he used the inner part of it as an office. Or perhaps he lived there, for whenever I knocked on the door of his house and it was opened to me by Mrs Hamper (a gaunt ratty woman very like Samuel Whiskers' wife Anna Maria), the exchange would be the same ...

'Oh, good morning. Is Mr –'

'Round the back.'

And round the back I would go, across the yard, into the first sty, and duck low beneath the doorway to find Mr Hamper inside, in a sitting position. Somewhere underneath him, that is to say, there was a long-suffering chair, but his bulk overflowed and concealed it. The only other furniture in this sparsest of business premises was a rickety table upon which stood two thick pint glasses and a fat black bottle. Here the conversation was also standard, regardless of the time of day.

'You'll take a drink, young man?'

My reply evolved, from an initial 'That's very kind of you' through 'Well, it's a bit early (or late) for me' to 'No, not for me, thanks, Mr Hamper', but the outcome was always the same, since no dealings in the stock market were ever permitted until my glass had been filled and emptied. Only then would he lever himself up with a grunt and allow me to make my wobbly way out of the sty to view what pigs he had on offer.

Mr Hamper kept Saddleback sows and crossed them with a Large White boar (that might have been his brother) to produce a very useful sort of blue-and-white pig. Over the years I bought a great many slips from him, and always when we shook hands at the end of a deal I thought I had had the best of it. True, I had to pay his price. But where would I find a better bunch of pigs? Or a pleasanter man to deal with? Well worth a bit extra. That's what a pint of parsnip wine does for you.

Eventually I deserted Mr Hamper for a dealer called Alfred Easy, who never offered me a glass of anything, and found for me, more cheaply, pigs of a lesser quality. And he in his turn became redundant when, after five years or so, I was in a position to breed my own requirement of store pigs.

Molly, the first sow, was a pedigree Large White. Early on I had had pipe-dreams of establishing a herd ('Bath & West Champion comes, yet again, from the world-famous Woodlands Large Whites'), but, as time passed, decided to do as the rest of the Romans and stick to the local practice of putting the Wessex Saddleback sow, an outlying pig and a good mother, to a Large White boar. This cross resulted in a sensible trouble-free sort of pig that grew on well to pork or bacon.

But before I got to that stage, while still at the tender mercies of Hamper or Easy, Molly used to go by trailer to a boar at the other end of the village, and would then produce, three months, three weeks, and three days later, a fair number of pigs and do them well. She kept this process up, twice a year, a model mother, until while still in her prime she managed to break a leg out in The Wood, and had to be slaughtered.

Quiet and biddable as she usually was, Molly had seemed to me the ideal subject for an experiment in pig management in the shape of tethering. I bought a very expensive piece of equipment that I had seen attractively advertised, consisting of a complicated harness of the best leather, attached by an arrangement of chains and springs to a kind of anchor driven deep into the ground.

Molly submitted, almost without protest, as Gladwyn and I trussed her up in a positive web of straps and buckles, and then condescended to walk, like a huge dog on a lead, to the chosen spot. The tether was clipped on to the harness, and we stood back.

For a few minutes Molly rootled around, the chain lying slack, the spring unstretched. But in due course she came, first literally and then metaphorically, to the end of her tether. Finding herself restrained by some unknown agency, she gave a loud squeal of fury and put out all her strength. The mighty anchor stood firm, the strong spring expanded but a little, the stout cable tautened and held her tight.

'You're wasting your time, old girl – that chain would hold a battleship!' I shouted above the squealing. And with that the beautiful leather strapping all burst like so much binder twine, and Molly galloped angrily into the sunset, the tattered remains of the wonderful patent pig-harness flapping forlornly against her sides.

Molly's replacement was a Saddleback, and by the autumn of 1953 there were four living in the Wilderness hen-houses, and trailer rides up the village were becoming altogether too much of a performance. I needed my own boar.

In those days before the introduction of the Landrace, there was no breed to touch the Large White for bacon production, and when I saw two six-month-old boars advertised locally, I rang up a farmer friend and asked him to come over with me to have a look at them. I suspected that his head was a little leveller than mine. I did not want to buy a pig in a poke.

It is a most pleasant and comfortable thing, to hang over the wall of a sty and look upon pigs. Any kind of pig is of interest, but people who work with stock learn to tell quality; and the two young boars whose backs were scratched that October morning were a picture.

Litter brothers, they stood shoulder to shoulder and grunted their appreciation of our fingers in the coarse hair of their long strong backs. Their fringed ears stood stiff, their tails curled tight, and the white lashes lay thick on their closed eyes as they swayed like belly-dancers to our touch. The price was right, the bystanding breeder reliable. All I had to do was choose.

There was nothing in it. Lord knows they had length and to spare. But perhaps one was a shade longer than his brother, and I leaned over and gently pulled his ear.

'What d'you reckon, Peter? Which would you pick?'

'There's very little in it, Dick. Perhaps the one you're touching is a shade longer than his brother.'

Maybe the one we left behind also had a happy and memorable life, but I'm glad I didn't take him. I'm sure he could never have been the pig that Monty was.

Something-or-other Field Marshal was his registered name, so he had to be called after that self-important little soldier. But everything about my Monty was big – his heart, his appetite, and eventually his size. Once he became too large to get into my pig-weighing machine, there was no way to gauge his weight but by eye, but before his last illness, five years later, I reckon he would have topped 600 pounds.

By that time he had had for a long while a harem of ten Saddleback sows, roaming the dells and hillocks of The Wood. And always, when one happened suddenly upon him around a bush, or saw him come crashing through the undergrowth at the cry of 'PIG-pig-pig-pig!' and the rattle of the bucket, there would be an instant of shock at the sheer bulk of him. The sows were hardly sylph-like, but when Monty covered one, it seemed that her back must break.

Yet he was the gentlest of animals. Like all his kind, he loved to be scratched, but he had two particular penchants in the matter. He liked it done on the top of his head, between his great ears; and he liked it done while he was sitting down. Perhaps in the belief that it made things easier for the scratcher, though in fact the reverse was true, he would lower his hams, place his forefeet neatly together, and sit bolt upright, eyes already closing in anticipation.

If the children were playing in The Wood and came upon him, Monty would immediately sit to attention. And though the girls could reach the tickling spot without too much difficulty, Giles at the age of four or five had to reach right up, his nose level with the boar's tusks, his face almost touching the huge snout.

A diary entry in 1959 tells the end of the story:

Thursday 28 May
Monty died in the small hours. Shall miss him, having had him five years, seven months. Vet did post mortem – constipation due to eating earth.

I hadn't liked the look of him on the Wednesday and was worried enough to seek professional advice, but was not at all expecting what I found on the Thursday morning.

Behind the back doors of the barn was a square area, fenced of course with coffin boards, which led by way of a narrow passage directly to The Wood, and thus allowed us to move pigs between one place and the other. In the centre of this square was a hollow, the bed of an old pond. Like some African water-hole it was often bone dry, and the sows would lie on its slopes and enjoy the sun like fat ladies at the seaside. Sometimes, in the wet, it had a lovely muddy mess in it and became a wallow.

That morning there was only one animal lying stretched out on the bank of the pond. For a second I thought that Monty was simply sleeping. But somehow he seemed flattened, almost two-dimensional like a great cardboard figure, and even longer than in life. Later, when the vet cut him open, the endless length of his gut was chock full of earth, like a giant sausage. Some depravity of appetite had led him to eat the mud of the wallow until at last he was bunged up solid. Not much of a death.

I have one splendid memento of Monty, a photograph of him in his prime, taken by a press photographer who had come to interview me for an article in a local paper. Majestically, the boar sits on his great backside, and, respectfully, I squat before him on my haunches, my fingers making their customary obeisance upon his bristly brow. Some pig.

Of course there were plenty of other, lesser, casualties. Small pigs often died of what we called 'the thumps', a lung condition caused by an infestation of worms. And there were accidents. A slip drowned in one of the old baths that were used as drinking-troughs.

Most losses were from overlaying. In the first days after farrowing, piglets are always at risk. Even the most careful of mothers, getting up or going down with all the caution at her command, cannot alter the fact that she is about a hundred times as heavy as one of her newborn children. And, squashing apart, sometimes she will accidentally step on one so weightily that the sharp hoof will slice it beyond repair.

There are devices for the babies' protection – farrowing rails for them to shelter behind, creeps for them to withdraw into, crates to contain their mothers, but as a rule the early part of a piglet's life is hazardous. Maybe it doesn't prove anything, but the times when we never lost babies were when a sow farrowed completely naturally out in The Wood.

She would make a huge nest, the size of a small room, out of bracken and coarse grasses and twigs and all sorts of other vegetation, always choosing a well-sheltered spot. I remember going out one morning of heavy frost, and all The Wood was white but for one place. It was under a bank that kept the wind away and beneath a big evergreen that would hold the rain off later, there was this enormous bird's-nest in which a contented mother brooded a crowd of newborn piglets all as warm as toast.

But motherhood isn't always so idyllic, and when things go amiss it can be nightmarish.

Somewhere in the time between Molly's death and Monty's arrival, I bought two hilts (the local name for gilts, or maiden sows) of the Gloucester Old Spots breed. Called the cottage pig, the Gloucester Old Spots had a reputation for doing well on poorish fare, and was much used for tidying up the fallings of West Country orchards. Gladwyn must have had a hand in the naming of these two sisters for they were called Olwen and Blodwen. I mated them to a Spots boar.

When Olwen farrowed, she couldn't have been less trouble. She was placid, careful, and sensible, the epitome of a good mum. Two days later it was Blodwen's turn.

I had looked at her last thing at night and she hadn't started, but when she did, the scream that woke us was the one and only noise to be made by her luckless firstborn.

I don't know for sure why, rarely, sows will kill and eat their young. Almost always, when it does occur, it's the animal's first litter, and in her excitement or bewilderment she may pick up a piglet in her mouth. If she breaks the skin and tastes blood, it's chomp chomp. By the time I got there, number one was vanishing down Blodwen's throat, and number two was on its way out to what promised to be an extremely short life. I yelled for Myrle, and we passed the next hours in a drill demanding co-operation and speed.

Blodwen lies down, out comes a piglet, and Myrle

shoves the head of a yard-broom in the sow's face while I dash in, grab the baby, and dash out again.

By morning we had seven survivors in a basket, but every attempt to re-present them to Blodwen was met with murderous fury. Some we tried to foster on to gentle Olwen, but they did not survive the competition. And two we put with Anna, who came smartly into milk at sight of these needy babies; but unlike dachshund puppies, newborn piglets have needle-sharp teeth, and Nanny had to retire hurt.

Quite often there would be a runt in a litter. They are called by different names in various parts of the country – cads, wasters, nesslegrafs, there are many terms. Round us they are dags. And the dag would be at risk throughout its usually short life. If it survived the competition and managed to avoid being overlaid, we might run it on, especially in a small or depleted litter, but the smallest and spindliest we put down. If however a dag made it to weaning age and had got reasonably plump, we might accord it the ultimate accolade, and ask our friends round to meet it, roasted and bearing in its little jaws an apple speared with cloves.

Once a year the butcher came and killed a bacon pig for our own needs. Everything about a pig is of use, they say, except the squeal, though we never could face the trotters. In Tytherington days I had once lodged at a pub where I took my meals with the landlord, whose favourite food was pig's trotters. He was a surly, shambling, soap-shy man with a glass eye, and he ate the pig's feet with a big horn-handled clasp-knife, spearing each one and holding it upright to gnaw and lick meditatively at it while the grease put a shine on his chin.

On the first occasion that we ate together I supposed that the tumbler of water that stood beside his pint pot of cider was a chaser, but not so. With a deft pinch of finger and thumb, out came that glass eye from its socket and plopped into the water to leer knowingly at me throughout the meal.

So trotters were out, and so was chitterling, but Gladwyn loved both. And the heart and the lights and a whole host of oddments went into the cats and dogs, even unto the tail.

A pig's tail hung upon the wall of the old disused sty where we mixed up their food. I had once gone to feed a pen of big baconers to find that there had been a bit of an argument where someone had got right down to the root of the matter. I picked the trophy off the floor and nailed it up, and it hung there for years, looking just like the bell-pull of Owl's that Pooh noticed after Eeyore's accident.

It was the perfect emblem of the whole business – the ultimate end of the pig.

Chapter 8

GRANDMOTHERS AND GRANDFATHERS

Saturday 15 May
Foot bad (Ben-the-bull stood on it yesterday while he was serving Strawberry). Gave myself the day off.
Into Bristol with M this morning. M bought two right shoes.
Granny K-S's funeral in afternoon.
In evening I left broody hen off eggs for two hours. Bloody fool.

I was very close to my four grandparents and they were all important to me in my childhood. Two of them lived very near, two in South Wales. To visit the latter meant a journey from Bristol to Cardiff, by rail through the

Severn Tunnel, whereas I could walk to my father's parents' house in ten minutes. So I'll begin with them, the closest.

Grampy K-S had married a girl called Alice Keep whose family firm, Keep Brothers, were importers and exporters, Birmingham-based. Despite that thin trickle of Charles II's blood, we were, the Victorians would have said, 'in trade'. More of Granny K-S in a moment (and there was more of her too), but first more of Father's father. He was a small slight man, who had lost most of his hair when I first came to know him and sported a drooping scrubbing-brush sort of a moustache, the middle of which was stained by the nicotine of many cigarettes. He was a Methodist by religious persuasion and a teetotaller, whether by choice or because of his faith I don't know. Every morning there would be, for family, any guests and all the servants (cook, housemaids, parlour maid) morning prayers in the big dining-room of the large imposing house called, by virtue of its position high above the village, Bitton Hill.

I'm making Grampy K-S sound a bit boring, but he wasn't in the least. There were twinkly blue eyes behind his pince-nez, and he loved jokes, especially feeble jokes, and the best sort of puns (which are bad ones). Setting out for a nearby suburb of Bristol he might say, 'I'm on my way to Warmley.' Pause, a sort of giggle, and then, 'I shan't go as far as Chile.'

Sometimes, perhaps for a birthday, he would write me a

letter, always ending: 'Yr affec G Father, Chas King-Smith'. And affec he was, I know now, though never demonstrative, and I remember with pleasure the things we enjoyed together, just he and I, away from Granny K-S's all-embracing presence. We would quite often, in the school holidays, play golf together, I in my mid-teens, he in his late sixties. I would hit the ball long distances, but seldom in the right direction. Grampy would drive straight down the middle, no more than a hundred yards probably and progress to the green in similar fashion. I don't remember ever beating him.

Once we made a never-to-be-forgotten expedition together, just the two of us. He was a keen lepidopterist, with a huge collection of beautifully mounted specimens of butterflies and moths, kept in a handsome walnut cabinet with dozens of shallow drawers, and I, inspired by him, was a keen butterfly-hunter. What drew me was the thrill of the chase, dashing, net in hand, after the fluttering jinking insect and, with luck, catching it with one well-aimed swish. Grampy had an enormous variety of different types of butterflies and moths in his collection, though of course there were several native species that he had never caught. One of these was a little dingy brown butterfly called the Lulworth Skipper, first found at Lulworth Cove in Dorset in 1832. In 1932, Grampy and I set out to catch one.

At that time he owned a squarish rather upright motor car called a Clyno, which I'm sure was capable of travelling at more than thirty miles per hour, but not in Grampy's hands, for he never exceeded this speed. So the journey from Bitton Hill to Lulworth Cove must have taken a good many hours, but we arrived at last and set off, nets in hand, around the steep heathery slopes. On that warm summer's day, there were plenty of butterflies about, but nothing that looked remotely like our quarry.

Then, just as we were about to give up and return to the Clyno for the long slow journey home, I saw a little dingy brown butterfly flittering about among the heather tufts, and I rushed after it and swung my net and caught it! Cautiously Grampy, a man so gentle that he would not have harmed a fly, transferred the captive from net to stink-bottle, wherein it quickly died.

'Is it?' I panted.

'Yes,' he answered, 'it is a Lulworth Skipper! Well done!'

I had come. I had seen. I had conquered!

He was a lovely old chap, was Grampy K-S. I doubt if

ever, in his long life, he raised his voice in anger. I don't remember that he ever addressed his wife as Alice or that she ever called him Charles. Instead, they always used the names that Father's generation of the family had saddled them with. He was Potie, she was Motie.

Granny K-S spoiled me rotten and nothing was too good for me. What one first noticed about her was her face, pink-complexioned, unlined, almost childlike including the baby-blue eyes, even in her sixties. She wore her white hair scraped back and done in a bun. Her clothes, it seemed, were always the same – a pale-coloured blouse and a skirt of a khaki shade. Ankle-length the skirt always was, so that the sight of her feet was the only proof that she had legs. Whatever her shape may have been as a young woman, she was now pear-shaped, as though gravity had caused everything to drop. Outdoors, on the croquet lawn, let's say, she always put on (whatever the weather) a long coat with a kind of feather-boa collar, and fastened to her hair with long pins one or other of a collection of large ornate hats.

I have a photograph of her dressed thus, in the company, believe it or not, of the wife of King George V. During the war, Queen Mary was staying with the Duke of Beaufort at Badminton (where she supervised a gang of men whose sole work was to pull the ivy – which she hated – from every building, wall or tree) and she came one day to inspect the Golden Valley Paper Mills. One of Granny

K-S's long-held, but seemingly quite impossible, dreams was to pour tea for Queen Mary one day. That now she did, in the Mill canteen. What a pair they must have made, both wearing enormous hats, one regal, one very respectful yet in her way equally majestic, both as tough as old boots.

Granny K-S wore the same uniform for church (C of E for her), where I was usually expected to accompany her. During the sermon she would feed me glycerine pastilles. Despite her sweetly gentle appearance, she was the complete matriarch. To see her sitting at the head of the very large dining table – at Sunday tea, say, when there might be fourteen or even twenty of us on parade – you knew you must mind your manners. The reward for good behaviour was a simple square of Bournville plain chocolate, dislocated from its large bar by the senior grandchild present, using one half of a pair of broken scissors, an instrument know as 'Pecker'.

Granny wasted nothing. No string was ever cut from a parcel, but always untied and re-coiled. The brown paper from that parcel would be carefully smoothed and folded for later use. When letters were received, their envelopes, if in good condition, were kept for service at a later date when they would be sealed by strips of sticky paper, carefully removed from the borders of sheets of stamps. When Sunday tea was over, and the men had gone to play billiards, the women to tend their small children, the larger

Grampy and Granny K-S

The hint of a smile on his face leads me to think he may have been composing one of his bad puns to try on the photographer. She has that gentle saintly look that disguises the fact that she ruled the roost.

Grampy B

One of the all-time greats of Welsh Rugby Union Football, A. W. Boucher. Welsh International and Barbarian, Captain of Newport Rugby Club. Another awful punster.

Granny B

I'd forgotten that she had that gap in her teeth. She was such fun.

Father 1916

I wore that Sam Browne belt of his in the next war.

Four generations 1926

From left: Granny B, Great-grampa Heard, Me (Mother (24)

Four generations 1997

From left: grandson Tom, great-granddaughter Josie, daughter Liz, Me

Me aged 2

Forgotten dog's name.
Note my hair-do.

Myrle aged 4

With spaniel, Jidd.

Me aged 9

About to set off for
the first term at
boarding school.
I don't think I was as
confident as I look.

Me aged 11, *with Raleigh*
Tourer with 3-speed
Sturmey-Archer gears.

Me aged 21

Somewhere in Italy 1943.

Myrle aged around 18

Me aged about 16

The first farmhouse
Woodlands Farm, hardly an example of architectura beauty.

Our wedding day in February 19

Susie

*Of the many lives. Something
of her essential toughness and
tetchiness shows through.*

My brother Tony

With his badger, Wilhelmina.

Jonah

*Properly known as Champion
Daggerwick Double Crown,
the first of Myrle's successes in
the show-ring.*

Monty

*Pig of pigs. I should by rights have been scratching him between
his big ears, but he quite liked his snout to be smoothed.*

Juliet's Christening

Back row: Grampy K-S, Myrle's mother, me, Mother, Father.
Front row: Granny K-S, Myrle with baby, Granny B.

The photographer's flash bulb had just exploded dramatically, staining the ceiling and making us all have eyes like currants.

Giles (6) and Liz (11) at school

Liz, me, Juliet

I'd just received an Honorary M.A. from Bath University.

Myrle and me

At Diamond's Cottage, around 1988, with Dodo, star of television, in undignified position.

At our olden Wedding in 1993

Giles, Liz, Juliet, Myrle, me.

Meeting Princess Anne

At the Guildhall. We are all grinning sycophantically, but I then had a spirited argument with her on the subject of pigs. I like 'em, she doesn't.

In Lizzie's garden for my 75th birthday party in 199

Standing: Charlie, Lucy, Dave, Liz, Juliet, Tony, Myrle, Clare, me
Duncan, Giles, Will, Kelly, Rachel, Josie, Tom.
In front: Tommy, Joe, Nat, Nina, Dan, Clare.

children to play croquet, and the maids had cleared away the plates empty now of salmon-paste sandwiches and biscuits and a variety of cakes, Granny K-S's heavy figure would be moving ponderously around the table, in her hands a wooden dustpan and a wooden brush. She carefully swept up every crumb from the cloth – 'For the birds, boykie' (as all grandsons were called). Even in the war, Granny always began her letters to me in Italy, 'My darling boykie'.

Croquet was an important part of the ritual at Bitton Hill. As a family, we liked playing games. There was a tennis court, and a clock-golf green, and there was the billiard room (children not allowed), but we played an awful lot of croquet. Granny K-S always played with the black ball and always sought to save it from being knocked away, by the red or the blue or the yellow, by pleading for it, as a mother might plead for her child's life: 'Oh don't hurt my little blackie, darling! Spare my blackie!' Which only resulted in us bashing the black ball away into the rhododendrons at every opportunity to the sound of Granny's plaintive cries.

An indoor game that was very popular was called Five Square. It consisted of making five-letter words, usually in the form of anagrams, by placing cardboard letters in a certain order as they are called (by the Caller, dipping into a bag – Granny K-S was always the Caller). Twenty-five letters were called in each game, making a matrix of five words across, five words down, thus five square. UESHO makes HOUSE, for example.

Certain combinations were tricky. Should one of us make ASTFR, it was always read out as RAFTS. Granny wouldn't have known the alternative (beginning with F), but she might have asked what it meant. How delighted we were when, sometimes, she herself made a combination of HERWO. She knew that one, and wouldn't speak it but simply point at it and say, 'Such a nasty word, darlings, but it's worth ten points.'

It's a great game, is Five Square. Far better than scrabble, and my wife and I still play at it against one another at teatime every day. Now of course we can make a number of very rude words of which Granny would never have heard.

However, there was one game that Granny and I played regularly, *à deux*, called *L'Attaque*. This was in essence a battle between an English army and a French one. Each army fielded a number of different ranks, thirty a side, I think, ranging from Field Marshal or *Chef d'Armée* to mere Privates. Each soldier was painted upon a little cardboard backing, standing in a metal foot. Each challenge between an English and a French soldier was decided by rank and of course each player could only see the backs of the opponent's troops.

I am not proud of the scheme I dreamed up, which meant that Granny always lost. First I established that I would always be English and she French. Then, secretly, I made very small distinguishing marks – a little x perhaps – on the backs of her more important officers, the *Chef d'Armée*, a general or two, the Colonels, so that I knew just the right soldiers to attack. I always won. Until one day Father came into the room as we were playing and – horror of horrors – stood behind me and watched as the battle progressed.

Afterwards, on the way home, he said to me, 'You marked her cards, didn't you, old boy?' And of course I had no option but to admit the truth. The next time we went to Bitton Hill together, he made me confess and apologize. I felt dreadful. Granny K-S only smiled her sweet smile, but I'm not sure we ever played *L'Attaque* again.

An abiding final memory is of a Sunday lunch, where Grampy K-S was carving a chicken – for so many of us that he must have thought about the miracle of the loaves and fishes as he teased out every shred of meat from the carcass. Chickens, hens rather, were always known to Granny as 'fowls'. A number lived in the orchard, and when they ceased to lay or simply became very old, they finished up on the dining-table. On this particular Sunday, as Grampy handed out the final plate of meat to the final family member, leaving only himself unserved, Granny K-S called down the table in her gentle voice, 'Potie dear, all the rest of the fowl is yours'. There was only the parson's nose left.

The Palm Tree

One August day as pleasant as can be
Father and I go down in company.
He on a walking stick with rubber tip
Supports a superannuated hip,
While, less infirm by twenty-seven years
Of scything Time, I bear a pair of shears
And pull a mower. We are come to shave
And clip and smarten up his parents' grave.

With very decent lack of haste we go
Down this, 'cross that, along another row,
And ruminate, as peacefully we pass,
Upon the people underneath the grass.
Adored, Revered, Devoted, Dearest, Best-
Beloved, rank on rank they lie at rest,
Strata of faces gazing, every one
Once warmed, towards this summer morning's sun.

Grandparents' grave is by a tropic tree,
A kind of hairy palm: a mystery
How such an interloper should aspire
To grow to grace a grave in Gloucestershire.
'I've booked the next-door space for me and Mum,'
Says Father. 'So that tree will have to come
Down to make room, or we'll be out of true.'
True. 'And I've never liked the thing, have you?'

A quarter of a century away
This grave was dug, round which I mow today
And tend and tidy. Twice that five-and-score
I have enjoyed, and he three times and more
Who puffs his pipe and leans against the stone
Of neighbours who will some time be his own.
'No, I don't like it.' On the other hand,
Let's hope, long may the hairy palm tree stand.

1972

Mother's parents lived in Glamorgan, in a village called Dinas Powis. Her father's name was Arthur Boucher. Her mother was born Frances Claribel Heard, though Grampy B's pet name for her was Dodo. Granny B was in many ways the opposite of Granny K-S, being smaller, neat instead of cumbersome, her face not pink but brown, not bland but etched with laughter lines. She was more worldly, had a sharper sense of humour and of the ridiculous.

She was one of the ten children (five boys, five girls) of William Esau Heard, who came from Appledore in Devon, settled in Newport, Monmouthshire, and after a long business career in shipping, died some months short of his 103rd birthday.

I have read the excellent speech he made at his 100th birthday party. 'The Grand Old Man of Newport celebrates his centenary', wrote the local newspaper, with a picture of Great-Grandpa Heard in morning dress, grey top hat on his head, his expression still alert above the long fine white beard.

Legend has it that he walked to his office until he was ninety, when my Great-aunt Alice became alarmed for her father's safety, because he crossed the roads without looking to left or to right. She rang up the Chief Constable. That evening the old man remarked upon the thoughtfulness of the police.

'Do you know, my dear,' he said, 'there was a constable waiting at the roadside who stopped the traffic and escorted me across.'

This service continued until the walk became too arduous, when he caught the tramcar. The tramlines ran past Winchester House, and each morning Great-grandpa would appear at the top of the steps in full fig, while Alice (his eldest) and Hilda (his youngest), clothes brushes in their hands, carefully groomed morning-coat and top hat. The tram waited until he had descended the steps in their care. At ninety-five he retired.

I have a splendid photograph of me (aged about four) and Mother and Granny B and Great-Grandpa Heard, at a family wedding in 1926. (Now, in the twenty-first century, I have another, of my great-granddaughter Josie and my grandson Tom and my daughter Lizzie and me, at a family party.)

William Esau Heard kissed me once, that I remember, on top of my head, when I was about six. I can recall my face being buried in that soft silky beard that smelt of an aromatic liquid called 'bay rum'.

One of the differences between Granny B and Granny K-S (both much of an age) lay in their mobility. Granny K-S was ponderous – moving about the croquet lawn, for instance – with slow measured steps, that long skirt dragging. Granny B's skirts were calf-length, and her movements quick: more, she would walk with us, to the common, to the village, whereas the other only ever left her house to ride to church in a motor car.

I don't think Grampy B ever learned to drive. Certainly the Bouchers never owned a car, so that when Tony and I stayed at Dinas Powis, we always went to the seaside by bus. Grampy B would go by train to his office in Cardiff, and Granny would take us on the bus to Barry Island to play on the beach and build sandcastles and bathe and eat sandy Marmite sandwiches and ice creams.

There was a boating-lake there, where they had little child-sized boats, each with a steering-wheel and an accelerator (I don't remember any way of braking). How those boats worked I don't know, but to pilot one of them, all on one's own, buzzing rather slowly round the lake like a waterborne dodgem, was magic.

We must always have gone to stay with the Boucher grandparents in the summer holidays, I think – I don't remember anything other than constant blue skies and sunshine on the beach at Barry Island, a very big beach, it seemed.

Fifty or so years later, I chanced to go back there.

It was really a rather small beach, and it was raining buckets.

The thing about Granny B was that she was always such fun to be with. Not a bad epitaph.

Grampy B, who adored her, was a big man, running to fat when I first remember him, as retired athletes do, with a head of white hair and a fine white moustache. He had been one of the all-time greats of Welsh Rugby Union Football.

Like Grampy K-S, he also much liked poor jokes, and his idea of fun, when, say, they came to us for Christmas, was to secrete about the house such things as a banana that squeaked, a doughnut that made rude noises as of one breaking wind, a fork that bent when you used it, and a realistic rubber dog-mess. Grampy K-S might have laughed at these items from the joke shop. Granny K-S would not have. Nor would she have found a rude postcard funny, but mercifully when she did actually receive one, she didn't understand it.

It was sent – from Tenby, of course – by Father's brother, my Uncle Joe (who had married Mother's younger sister, Rosemary). Joe would always send to Mother and Father one of Donald McGill's saucy postcards with pictures of fat ladies in bathing costumes and risqué captions. On one occasion my parents received a view of the North Beach and Goscar Rock.

'Surely this was meant for Motie?' they said. 'She must have got ours!' And my little brother was hastily dispatched to Bitton Hill, to arrive there before the postman.

He was too late. Granny K-S was puzzling over a McGill postcard featuring, among other things, an octopus and the joke line leaned heavily on a confusion between 'tentacles' and 'testicles'.

'Oh, boykie!' said Granny as Tony burst in. 'Can you explain this to me?'

My four grandparents would meet, perhaps once a year, at Bitton Hill at one of those huge Sunday teas, at which, in summer, there would be peaches from the walled garden and, in winter, crumpets oozing butter and sometimes a particular cake made to the recipe of a distant never-seen-by-me cousin and always bearing her name. Thus, 'Now who will have a piece of Nellie Green?' (Another cousin, never-forgotten-by-any-of-us, once drained her cup and said to Granny K-S, 'Delicious tea, Alice dear, is it Typhoo Tits?')

Yet neither pair of grandparents ever relaxed the formality of their address, one to the other. No Christian name was ever used, nor such nicknames as Motie and Potie. Granny K-S might say to Granny B, 'Another cup of tea, Mrs Boucher?' And the Bitton grandfather might ask the Dinas Powis grandfather, 'Another sandwich, Mr Boucher?' And vice versa.

It did not imply coldness, much less dislike, that 'Arthur', 'Clare', 'Alice' and 'Charles' were never used. For each couple respected and approved of the other, despite differences of character and outlook. Quite simply, they were Victorians.

Chapter 9

Foxes and Badgers

25 March
Annuciation of BVM
Lady Day.
Fox took broody in orchard. Shot at him.

As well as the cattle, the pigs, the goats, the hens, the ducks, Woodlands Farm was home to a variety of other animals. There were rabbits, a spotted variety called English, which I bred in various colours – black, blue, chocolate – supposedly for show, though I never showed one. The pinnacle of my success was to sell one really well-marked buck for twenty-five pounds, but at least the deep-freeze was kept well stocked. There were guinea-pigs: I did show one of these – it won Third Prize (in a class of three) and Betsy had two much loved mice called Fairy Snow and Ogre Daz. There were also guinea-fowl, foolish birds that sometimes drowned while drinking at a cattle trough. There were lots of dogs always, mostly Myrle's dachshunds and twice we had a Great Dane, and masses of cats to earn their livings in barn and byre.

One memorable tortoiseshell-and-white queen called Dulcie Maude had, in all, 104 kittens. One litter was born and reared in an old doll's pram stashed away in a loft, the babies nestling comfortably on a doll's pink eiderdown. I fixed a kind of box on the wall outside the kitchen door, in which we put scraps for cats. It was called the Mogamatic Fullpuss.

As well as my collection of domestic animals, there were of course wild ones too. The woodlands were a paradise for wildlife. There were seven acres that had been the site of nineteenth-century open-cast coal workings, a jumble of high hillocks and deep bowl-shaped hollows. Three of these acres, uninspiringly called The Wood, were thickly covered with trees, principally ash and scrub oak. The remaining four, known as The Brake, were more open, and consisted of patches of rough grass and of dozens of huge blackberry bushes.

Under the great armoured bushes lived rabbits. Myxomatosis was still a few years away, and these stub-rabbits (an old name for those that live in above-ground cover) used the giant briars as protection from their natural enemies.

Judging by the number of times we saw them strolling up our drive and cocking their legs on the bordering shrubs, there were plenty of foxes too.

Our relationship with our foxes contained an illogical blend of love and hate. 'A wise fox will never rob his neighbour's hen-roost' is an adage of some truth, and we liked to think that the occasional slaughter, as on the day after Betsy's birth, was the work of an outsider. And generally the losses were small. The odd duck might go missing, and now and again a hen would 'steal' a nest – lay and sit a clutch of eggs in the bottom of a hedgerow – and chance her luck, which then ran out.

On the whole, we took good care to shut the poultry up at night, and didn't grumble too much. Later we converted the loft over the old stables into a deep-litter house where three or four hundred birds lived in complete safety. But, before that happened, we were treated to a prime example of the kind of fox behaviour that leaves the farmer fuming.

I can remember the scene vividly, Before and After.

Before – a bunch of a couple of dozen cockerels foraging in spring sunshine on a patch of ground behind the cowshed. They were White Wyandottes, brilliant against the new grass, each wattled head capped with a rose-comb of brightest red. They're fit to kill, I thought as I went indoors to breakfast. They were.

After – a tremendous noise and kerfuffle had me dashing back out again with my mouth full. One of the many dachshunds that we then had was a chicken chaser – it's Mandy, I thought. As I came round the corner of the cowshed, I could see, dotted over perhaps half an acre of land, snowy-white bodies, still or still twitching, while the gaping survivors lurched about, shocked into shaking aimlessness. I counted. Sixteen dead. The raider had not been hungry, just having a bit of fun, for when I collected up the corpses, only one rose-combed head had been taken away, as a memento.

Woodlands Farm was on the outermost edge of a famous fox-hunting country, a land ruled by a great duke and his duchess. Twice only did we have the doubtful pleasure of the hunt's uninvited presence.

On one occasion a section of the field galloped through a number of electric-fenced paddocks, leaving a tangle of broken wire and uprooted posts. If they were shocked, they did not show it.

And on another memorable morning the duchess herself came clattering up the drive flanked by a couple of outriders, and galloped into the yard where a number of small children, our own and some of friends, were wandering about. 'Alas, regardless of their doom, the little victims play!' Luckily she missed them.

Oh, but only think of all the time when one fails to make a proper response. Remember those moments of inertia while the mind searches feverishly for the right riposte, witty or withering.

'Have ye seen hounds?' shouted the duchess with a sidelong glance from her side-saddle, but answer came there none. Open-mouthed the peasants stood while the riders pressed on and away, past our Dutch barn and across our pastures. As they disappeared beyond the horizon we heard a splintering crash. One of our five-barred gates had been broken, as a memento.

I don't want to moralize on the rights and wrongs of fox-hunting. There are reasons why the fox should not be a protected species. In those days the protection that the Woodlands foxes enjoyed during a season of hate was due to my poor marksmanship. But it's worth remembering the loving side of the relationship. The fox is a beautiful animal. His colouring is beautiful, varying from a mahogany to a red so pale as almost to be orange. And there is beauty in his moving, not drip-tongued, drop-eared, draggle-tailed and half a field in front of thirty couple of hounds, but in the full joy of his freedom, drifting across the ground as light as a hen's feather, his brush fluffed, his ears cocked, and his sharp eyes bright.

Early one fine morning I drew the bedroom curtains and there he sat on the lawn below, front paws neatly together, white-tipped brush curled around him, muzzle pointed enquiringly up to my window. I don't remember my reaction, can't recall if it was hate – get the gun – or love. What a picture. I only know that when I walked out into the empty garden, there upon the steps of the sundial was a steaming pile of fresh scats, as a memento.

Our ambivalent attitude towards foxes didn't apply to our badgers, because they did our livestock no harm. Not that they would have turned their snouts up at our birds if a fowl-house door had been left open one night, but it just didn't happen. The only damage they did was occasionally to roll in standing corn, leaving billiard-table-sized playpens of thoroughly flattened stalks.

The badgers lived in The Wood. One of the large mounds held a complex of rooms and tunnels driven perhaps ten feet deep under the roots of a little grove of elder and holly, the bark of several of the trees scored vertically by the cleaning of long front claws, and the ground around worn bare and smooth by the passing of many feet over many years. The sett had seven entry holes, and the colony, we judged, was a large one, perhaps of several families living communally. Sometimes we were wakened from deep sleep by the racket going on in The Wood, two boars wrangling maybe, or cubs at mock-fighting play, a cacophony of high-pitched staccato squeaks and chattering.

At about this time my brother, Tony, had a pet badger called Wilhelmina. She had been given to him as an orphaned cub: a little sow with a particularly wide strip of white down the centre of her face, a stripe so wide as to distinguish her for ever from all other badgers.

She was just like a little bluish kitten, probably no more than ten days old. This extreme youth may well have been significant as regards her reactions. Later I heard the story of another, older, cub that was given to a doctor who was crazy about badgers. It lived in his garage beside his car, and was at all times ill-humoured, guaranteed to bite everyone and anyone. Denied this pleasure by evasive action, it eventually contrived to make use of a handy pair of steps to climb in through the open window of the car, which it then eviscerated, ripping the interior to small shreds.

Wilhelmina by contrast was biddable, intelligent, and affectionate. She used her teeth, but only in love-bites. Standing upright, so that once she was part-grown gumboots were no defence, she would bite Tony in the fleshy part of the back of the thigh just above the knee, first in one leg, then in the other.

At first it was all hard work, bottling such a small baby. And in the early days he must have worried that once she was really mobile, she would light out for the wild, and he trained her to a lead. But it wasn't necessary. She reacted in every way like a domestic animal, though the nocturnal habits of her species caused her to be sleepy by day and only really to be wakeful towards evening.

At that time my brother lived with our parents, now removed to Bitton Hill, a large Victorian house that had plenty of outbuildings, and Wilhelmina slept her days away in a small loose-box that had once been home to a donkey.

But as soon as Tony arrived back from work, the badger would chatter like a magpie until let out, to greet him with the double bite, and then to rush off with the terriers for a game on the lawns that could only be called rough-and-tumble. Accepted entirely by the dogs, Wilhelmina would knock them flying and they'd return the compliment and not a harsh word was spoken.

By the time she was eighteen months old, Wilhelmina was sleeping in an old coach-house where my grandfather had kept his wood-turning lathe, and she was free to come and go during the night. Unfortunately this meant that others were free to come in, and at her first season a big boar badger sought her out. It was not her sexual condition that excited him, rather was he offended by her state of domesticity and her treacherous alliance with man. He gave her a terrible beating, and nearly killed her.

Wilhelmina recovered and, in due course, came on heat for the second time. And now she left for good to seek her wild fortune, and the stable yard never heard that magpie chatter again.

Two years later, Tony was driving home late at night, going fast up the long winding drive to the house. He saw the badger that suddenly crossed the road, but, try as he would, could not avoid it. It was a sow, with a stripe down its face so wide as to distinguish it for ever from all other badgers.

My closest contact with a badger at Woodlands Farm was of a nature so unlikely as to be unbelievable. Many years ago I put the incident down on paper and sent it off to a journal called *The Countryman*. I did not even receive the courtesy of a note of rejection.

It was my morning to milk, a peerless morning towards the end of June. Going out to fetch the cows, my way lay across a seven-acre field called The Big Ground. This had been cut for hay the previous day, and the tight uniform swathes of grass lay bluish and shining in the risen sun. Suddenly, out in the middle, I saw a badger. By chance I had no dog with me that might harry it, so I ran, fast, to see if I could get a closer look before the brock could leg it away to the safety of the bordering Brake. Not only did it not run away, it took not the slightest notice of my panting arrival, but continued to snuffle about in the cut grass with as much unconcern as though I had still been in bed. It seemed the most comprehensive snub. Embarrassed, I took off my hat and with it patted the broad bottom. I began to murmur inanities.

'Hullo, old chap! What's the matter then? Don't you speak to strange men? Sent me to Coventry, have you?'

But indeed this was the unkindest cut of all. The badger would not in any way acknowledge my presence, it simply moved, achingly slowly, towards the shelter of the woodland, my hat beating an unavailing tattoo on its backside. It found a hole in the hedge and disappeared.

Two mornings later, at the very same time in the very same place, I saw two badgers. With the nonchalance and *élan* of a man on hat-slapping terms, I ran gaily towards them. My friend, I thought! And his friend! Asinine words formed themselves ready for my smiling parted lips. 'Hullo again! Wanting some more of the same treatment, old fellow? And have you brought your girlfriend?' But at a short hat's throw from the pair, it became suddenly obvious that this was a case of mistaken identity. With a horrid chorus of noises, squeaks, chatterings, and fierce piggy grunts, all unmistakably menacing, both badgers rushed madly at me on their short legs with mouths agape, and my camaraderie was forgotten as I fled at top speed.

It's a perfectly true story. But you can't really blame the editor of *The Countryman*.

Chapter 10

Dogs

Wednesday 3 January
Wonderful surprise! Susie returned after eight days and eight nights missing in this v. cold weather. Very weak and thin but OK. Obviously has been stuck somewhere. M. feeding her hourly with milk and glucose.

We've owned so many dogs over the years, but two unforgettable individuals at Woodlands Farm were Anna the dachshund and Susie the terrier. Anna's speciality was maternal love. Very early on, her name was usually corrupted to 'Nanny', and the sight of any nursling brought her running. You could hear the crackle of her starched apron as she fussed and fidgeted, certain of the incompetence of the real mother, of whatever breed, and longing to get her paws on the little darlings.

And it wasn't only puppies that she tried to foster. Kittens were well received in a cat crisis. She did not need to be in milk, she just came into it at the drop of a baby – as when she did her best for Blodwen's two piglets.

Her other *tour de force* was in holding her water. She may have been a bit short for a dachshund but she must have had a very long bladder because, in wet weather, which she abhorred, she would lie doggo for twenty-four hours. Chucking her out in the rain did no good, since you could not make her do anything. In fact it was a most unwise move, because her resulting wet feet went straight upstairs and on to the nearest bed.

'Have you seen Nanny anywhere?'

'No, but it's raining.'

'Oh well.'

And we would know that under one or other eiderdown there would be a small unmoving lump, in instant hibernation. But she wasn't a lie-abed in good hunting weather. Then she went to ground, often in company of Susie, after rabbit or badger or fox. She sometimes spent so long in the bowels of the earth that the search party would be called out, Myrle and I and the children and Gladwyn roaming the woods and fields, endlessly shouting her name, a fruitless exercise since she never answered to it.

The only hope of finding the needle in the haystack was to happen upon that day's chosen spot and hear her, only faintly at that because her bark was shrill and feeble. Once she was gone for forty-eight hours. We had drawn a complete blank at all the usual places, the big sett and favourite earths and buries in the woods and round various fields, the long densely bushed embankment of the railway that ran along Woodlands Farm's southern boundary. Fearfully we searched the tracks, and then the verges of the main road, but found nothing. We'd pretty well given up.

On the morning of the third day, Myrle said, 'I'm going to try to make my mind quite empty, and see what comes into it. Don't say anything.' And she shut her eyes. After a minute she said, 'She's in The Little Ground.'

The Little Ground was a two-acre piece of grass at the bottom of the farm, seldom frequented by dogs. I was sceptical but luckily said nothing. For as we walked across it, there, right in the middle, was a freshly dug rabbit bury, and coming from it a familiar squeaking.

It wasn't even a proper hole, just a deeper than usual version of the nest burrow or 'stop' that an outlying doe makes to have her kittens in; and by lying flat and reaching in to the full extent of my arm I could just grab hold of Anna's tail. I pulled her out, plastered in earth, and on our knees as though to give thanks for this safe delivery, we prepared to greet her. She gave herself a shake, and without a glance at us, went straight back down.

The story of Susie's entombment is much more horrific, but then the story of Susie's life consists of a series of incidents each one of which would have killed a lesser dog.

Keats may have been half in love with easeful death, but Susie went the whole hog, head over heels. She began at a tender age. A French bulldog of my mother's took one look at her, picked her up by the neck, and shook her like a rat. Bulldogs are undershot, and lock on, and by the time Susie was rescued, the bite had pierced the salivary gland. This in due course festered, and the sepsis looked likely to put an early end to her. However to the surprise of the vet, she survived this first, and, had we known it, comparatively minor brush with the last enemy.

All her subsequent attempts upon her own life took place at Woodlands Farm. Not long after we moved in, Susie sampled a different kind of poisoning. This time it was strychnine. How or where she came upon the bait that I suppose someone had put down for foxes we didn't know, but the vet knew what it was.

'I'm afraid there's no hope for her,' he said. Foolish man, he learned better as time went on.

The next two clashes were with motor vehicles. Ken the

builder drove up the yard one morning, and as he swung on to the concrete apron outside the dairy, Susie ran out of the door and under the van.

'Oh my God, the wheel went right over her, I felt the bump!'

Don't worry, Ken, I should have said. It'd take more than a potty little ten-hundredweight to do her in. And sure enough she didn't seem to have turned a hair let alone broken a bone, but simply growled with her customary surliness and went about her business. But that must have given her ideas, for the next car she tackled, quite soon afterwards, was a really big one, going fast, on the main road.

A friend who was staying had strolled down to the bottom of the drive with the dogs, when suddenly to her horror Susie dashed (cat perhaps?) straight across the road and under a speeding car. But there was no battered body left behind. Instead, fifty yards further on, just before the car disappeared from sight around the bend, out from beneath the chassis tumbled one small dog.

I can only suppose she must somehow have been caught up in the track-rods, and this time it must have given her a little bit of a fright because she ran home with her tail between her legs. She was a bit sore, a bruise or two perhaps, and snarled more than usual for a couple of days.

On Boxing Day 1950, Susie went missing. The search party found nothing, and darkness fell with no sign of her.

Anna's longest disappearance had been in fine summer weather, but now there was a bitterly cold spell with a biting east wind. On the whole we hoped she had gone to ground somewhere. At least she would be warmer down below.

At first this seemed the most likely explanation, since it was the thing she was keenest to do and had so often done. The alternatives were that she had been stolen – pretty unlikely: it would have had to be a bold dog-thief with stout gloves – or, more probably, run over by car or train. Two sides of Woodlands Farm carried this hazard, for the main Bristol to Chipping Sodbury road ran along its eastern edge, and the Paddington to South and West Wales line along its southern.

But though we hunted and rooted and poked about in every conceivable spot, and lay and listened long at every known hole in the ground, the year turned and 1951 came in with Susie lost to us at last.

Myrle said, 'I think you've got to resign yourself to the fact that your dog has almost certainly been killed.'

All the dogs were 'our' dogs, but the rest gave fealty to Myrle as food provider, trainer, and someone who could be guaranteed to treat them with patience and understanding. However my intolerant shouting and cursing at any show of disobedience seemed to appeal to Susie's cross-grained nature. Not that she ever had any soft answer to turn away my wrath: she simply snarled; but she must have sympathized with my quirkiness, because she followed me everywhere about the farm. At ploughing especially she would trot all day long up the bed of each new-turned furrow, exactly a yard behind the tail of the plough, waiting at the headland for the lift and turn and drop, and then back again down the other side of the 'land'.

'Well, I suppose she's had a pretty good run for her money. But I shan't half miss her, bad-tempered little swine.'

'I mean, we've looked everywhere, haven't we? We've been to the police station. We've asked everybody round about. And if she's been run over, we'd surely have found her.'

'Yes. The most likely thing really is that she tangled with a badger or badgers in the sett in The Wood. After all, what does she weigh, twelve pounds? A big boar badger might go thirty pounds or more. And think of those jaws.'

'But we couldn't hear anything at the sett, could we?'

'Exactly.'

By the time that a whole week, of unrelenting freezing

temperatures, had gone by since Susie's disappearance, we had resigned ourselves to the certainty that she was a goner. We should have known better. Early on the morning of Wednesday 3 January, I opened the back door on my way out to milk, and there in the grey light was a creature half-crawling, half-walking up the yard.

Not even such a masochist as Susie could voluntarily have reduced herself to the state that she was in, her eyes right back in her head, her mouth full of earth and bits of wood, her rough black-and-white coat matted with dirt and her own dung. Probably she'd become wedged, perhaps between tree-roots, somewhere deep enough for the air temperature to be bearable, and had literally had to wait to become thin enough to break free.

Any normal dog would have died of dehydration. As it was, she seemed at her last gasp. But it wasn't her last, by a long chalk. By the end of that day she was back in good growling form. And a couple of days afterwards you wouldn't have known that anything untoward had happened.

At the beginning of April that year Susie fell in love. Now five years old, she had up to this time defied all my efforts, and they were assiduous, to breed from her. Time and again she was taken to eminently suitable little working terrier dogs. Nowadays it's the fashion to call them Jack Russells after the famous nineteenth-century sporting parson (though in fact he kept all shapes and sizes right up to Airedales), but Susie wasn't interested in any aspect of them. All they got for their pains were snaps and snarls. And once we even tried her with one of our dachshunds in a desperate effort to breed puppies of some sort from her, but Susie flew at him and he left the room in gentlemanly embarrassment, his long nose much out of joint.

So by that spring we had relaxed any normal vigilance during her season, confident that she was her own best contraceptive. No suitor now, we knew, would try that long-preserved virginity. Enter Boy Dugdale.

This animal, a newcomer to the district, had been seen about the farm often enough to merit a name; and though the academic side of Nancy Mitford's lecherous lecturer was not apt, one glance at this dog left no doubt that here was a satyr of the first order. Partly it showed in his constantly aggressive marking, the cocked leg held so high that you wondered how he kept his balance, and in his strong confident scratching of the grass with his hind feet. Partly it was his uncanny ability to appear suddenly out of nowhere, deaf to threats and always just beyond missile-throwing range; and to jump walls that seemed much too high, and squeeze through or under impossibly small places. No prison could hold him, you felt sure, nor was there – and he was later to prove this – any fortress which he could not storm.

But chiefly it was his general appearance that showed Boy Dugdale's licentiousness. A large hairy mongrel terrier, long-legged and always moving, it seemed, on tiptoe, he was short-coupled (this is to say, his hind feet seemed much too near to his forefeet), and carried a tail which curled so far over his back as almost to touch what little neck he had. Before all, his face wore by some accident a permanent voyeur's leer, one side of the mouth drawn up to expose teeth and tongue, giving an overall expression of uncontrollable lust. Under our now lax surveillance, there was nothing to prevent his meeting Susie.

'There's that horrible Boy Dugdale again. Where's Susie?'

'Oh she's around somewhere. I shouldn't worry.'

'She is five, you know. Not a good age for having a first litter.'

'Susie get herself lined? You joke. Anyway he's much too tall to manage, and she won't let him near her.'

But he wasn't, and she did.

This hideous blend of Robin Hood, Houdini, Lothario, and Priapus was Susie's true love come at last, and by the time I'd finished breakfast the knot was tied. Out in the paddock beyond the Dutch barn, they stood back to back, Dugdale having overcome the disparity in size by the judicious use of rising ground.

Susie faced me with a smug smile, while her anchored swain, fearful of retribution, grimaced more odiously than ever over his shoulder. The die cast, I left them in peace, a course of inaction that led Dugdale to infer my approval of the match, so that within the twenty-four hours he made assurance not double but treble sure.

So, at the end of the first day in June, Susie once more put her life in jeopardy. She sentenced herself to hard labour and, in the box beside our bed, there was nothing to show for it but her evident distress. The vet came in the small hours. This particular one was a large man with a stutter and a comfortable bedside manner, literally, as he sat upon it to do his work.

Myrle fortified him and herself with tea and gin alternately. I slept, my usual response to trying situations like travel in an aircraft or the birth of my children. I woke to find that the vet had delivered two very large, very dead puppies.

'I can't f-f-f-feel any more. I think the b-b-b-bitch should be OK now.'

'Oh sure, she'll be OK.'

'I'll go home and get f-f-f-forty winks and look b-back later.'

By the time he returned with the announcement that d-dawn had b-bust and with the ends of striped pyjamas peeping shyly beneath his trouser turn-ups, Susie had given birth to a small brown-and-white bitch puppy, the one and only child of her long life. We called her Semolina and in due course gave her to Gladwyn.

Semolina was so thickly covered in hair that you hardly knew which way she was going and I'm not at all sure that she knew, such a silly excitable creature she was. But in time she produced a nice sensible litter from which we had one back, a much-loved person called Dido, eventually to be killed by a badger.

Dido in her life was as equable as her grandmother had been cantankerous, and she in turn carried on the line. Father had one of Dido's daughters, Jilly by name, who lived to the age of nineteen (multiply that by seven!), and doubtless today there are many remaining descendants of Susie's only dalliance.

Boy Dugdale did appear once more, but this time after bigger game. Tina, the first of our Great Danes, was at the height of her season, and for absolute safety I shut her for the night in an unused chicken-house in the orchard. The door was stout and locked, the small high windows, hinged on their upper edges and opening outwards, were each secured with a turn-button.

When I went to let Tina out in the morning, I could see through the glass that Dugdale stood beside her, his head on a level with her elbow, his face a mask of unrequited desire. Beneath one of the windows the turn-button had been turned. Somehow he had stood upon his hind legs on top of the nest-boxes that projected outside the house, and reached up with one conjuror's paw to turn the catch. Somehow he must then have nosed the window far enough open for him to wriggle and scrabble and lever and haul himself up and through it, only to find that he had set his sights too high. I unlocked the door and out he rushed.

One last contemptuous cock of the leg against an apple tree, one final backward leer, and away over the hill he went on his unending quest. Perhaps he brooded on what must have been the totally novel experience of failure. Perhaps he simply took his insatiable libido to fresh fields. But we never saw Boy Dugdale again.

In the years that followed, the tenor of Susie's life became quite placid. In 1954 it is true, she suffered a minor mishap when, thinking she looked off colour, I took her rectal temperature, only to lose my grip on the end of the thermometer, which promptly disappeared inside her. Gingerly I drove her to the surgery for the vet to recover it.

'N-not b-b-b-broken,' he said, 'and n-normal.'

And in December 1959 she threatened us briefly with the nightmare of nine years before. But she'd only been ratting, for a modest thirty-six hours, under Dugdale's chicken-house.

It was in May of 1960, when rising fourteen years old, but active and crotchety as ever, that she finally bit off more than she could chew by trying conclusions with the Paddington to Fishguard express. The police rang me after she'd been missing for two days.

'You lost a small black-and-white terrier?'

'Yes.'

'They've just rung up from the Stoke Gifford depot. One of their maintenance men spotted it by the side of the line, above your farm. They've buried it, they said, made a proper grave. Perhaps you'd like to pop down to the depot and identify it?'

'Yes. Thanks.'

I didn't want to see her all broken, of course, but I had to know. And when I'd removed the cross that some kindly railwayman had made from two scraps of wood, and opened up the little mound of clinker and rubble at the edge of the sidings, there she was all right. I always believe

– it's the most likely explanation – that she was hunting a fox over the top of the embankment, and, being by now rather deaf, did not in her excitement hear the train.

But even all those hundreds of tons of thundering metal had not reduced her, as I so feared, to some pitiful pulp. She only had a bloody nose.

Chapter 11
PLEASURE AND PURSUITS

Friday 27 October
To Beagle Ball. Bed 5 a.m.
Saturday 28 October
Very ill. Early bed.

Youth may be a stuff that will not endure, but luckily nobody thinks much about that at the time. We were pretty pleased with life, the sort of life we had both always wanted to lead, the kind of work we had always wanted to do. And after work, there was play.

One pleasure was the pub-crawl.

'Ale, man, ale's the stuff to drink
For fellows whom it hurts to think.'

A pint of best bitter cost ten old pennies and the

breathalyser was a score of years away. Capstan, Gold Flake, Senior Service – three bob for twenty, and we sucked the smoke deep into our lungs without any governmental warning.

There was a crowd of us, much of an age, noisy certainly, foolish probably, happy to drink a bit too much beer on occasion and enjoy one another's company. We were not earnest and intense, we did not wish to set the world to rights. It hurt to think about the immediate past and we weren't prepared to start fretting about the future.

Myrle and her sister Pam were privileged to be driven by me on one such outing. A dozen or more of us had graced with our loud presence The Star, The Rose & Crown, and The Fleur de Lys. Now, last in the convoy of cars, I drove our dung-splattered Land Rover through the narrow winding lanes, next stop The Cross Hands.

Under my masterful hands the steering wheel spun like a dancer, the gears meshed effortlessly, the powerful engine roared. What matter that the others had a head start on us?

The heroes of boyhood possessed me, and it was Captain G. E. T. Eyston's fearless foot that thrust the accelerator pedal flat against the floor. Why worry that the road was shiny with recent rain? Segrave would steer through the skid, or Campbell control it. As for the curves and the corners, all were subdued and subjugated, nay, positively straightened out, as with deft unerring touch Tazio Nuvolari swung the mighty Maserati onward, ever onward. On his lips a song, his steady eyes raked the road ahead.

'For God's sake!' said Pam.

And Myrle, 'Please stop and let me drive.'

'Why, in Heaven's name?'

'You're going to have us all in the ditch.'

Silly frightened girls! 'For God's sake' indeed! There was a veritable god at the wheel, *a deus intra machina*!

Suddenly, inexplicably, the approaching left-hand bend became sharper. Like a coiling snake, it seemed to move and tighten upon itself, and before you could say 'Enzio Ferrari' the offside wheels of the Land Rover slid over the grass verge and settled with a giant splash into the deepest of ditches. I stalled the engine. Only the sweet song of running water broke the silence.

In turn we made the forty-five degree climb out of the nearside door. Last away, as the captain of the ship must always be, I turned to survey her listing and settling, her upperworks leaning tiredly against a stout hedge, the flood-tide bubbling beneath her starboard gunwales.

'Go and find a telephone,' said Myrle, tight-lipped.

When the rescuers came, back from The Cross Hands, it was not with a whimper but a bang. Up the lane from their cars they marched, bearing trays with glasses and bottles at the ready to fortify the castaways, and many hands made light work of righting the stricken craft. Into the ditch they merrily splashed, and perching happily in the thorn hedge they flipped the Land Rover upright and popped it back upon the road like a Dinky toy. And away we all went with the empties.

Going to the flicks was a weekly event, almost always by ourselves while Gladwyn sat in for us. Once only, while someone else looked after the children, we took him with us. I can't remember if the film was an uproarious comedy. It needn't have been, because many different stimuli would set him off, but I do recall the embarrassment of having every eye in a crowded cinema focused upon us as Gladwyn, more or less continuously, screamed and shrieked with maniacal laughter, the tears coursing down his cheeks.

Once, I wrote a musical, in partnership with a doctor friend. I composed most of the tunes and wrote all the lyrics, while Jimmy's main contribution was to play the piano. I can neither read nor write music, so I would sing each new song into a huge old-fashioned tape-recorder and then Jimmy would play them. This he could only do in something called three flats, a key in which I found it difficult to sing. So that when we performed a selection of the numbers in front of professionals, as we did on a couple of occasions, hoping to interest them, it must have sounded a bit odd.

The Canutopian, as I titled it, was the story of a rough-hewn Canadian cousin of a well-to-do English county family. He comes to stay on a visit and falls in love with the beautiful daughter of the house.

Not long before, Julian Slade had had a huge success with *Salad Days*, and our rather simple naïve composition was much of the same kind. Except that Slade succeeded and we failed. Still, we had a lot of fun doing it, tiring as it occasionally was, such as the evening when Jimmy and his wife arrived at Woodlands Farm at 9 p.m. saying blithely that they had secured for their small children a sitter-in who was willing to hold the fort until 2 a.m. And I had to get up to milk at 5.30 a.m. I still think that a lot of the songs were quite good, and the words weren't bad either. One of the numbers, I recall, was 'Time Is Ours to Spend'. We spent it pleasantly enough.

Twice a year we went to a hunt ball. One was the annual gathering of the beagling folk, exchanging breeches and tweeds and stout boots for formal evening clothes, and the mud of the ploughed field for the floor of the Pump Room or the Guildhall.

The other was much grander, and took place at the house of that great hunting duke, where gathered all the Nimrods of note from Gloucestershire and neighbouring counties with their hard-riding, hard-running or hard-wading wives (fox, hare, or otter – everybody chased something).

The house was in fact not large enough to hold such a field, and the actual dancing was done in a big cold marquee attached to one side of it. Glimpses were to be had, on the way to the lavatory perhaps, of the duke warming his coat-tails before his fireside among a select group of cronies in their coats of blue-and-buff or blue-and-yellow or pink or green. (Father, incidentally, rated the duke, whom he met through such bodies as the Gloucestershire Society, as slightly superior to Churchill and marginally below the Queen.)

This matter of dress, just after the war, was still of some import. For such a thing as the duke's ball white ties and tails were very much the proper thing for men. Some callow youths might come in dinner jackets, one or two even daring to wear a soft shirt. But I by chance possessed the correct garb, and so, for a time at least, wore it, though it was not suited to my figure. It shows to its best on tall, slim, long-necked fellows. And the wearing of my particular clothes was made even less fetching by the fact that they had belonged to my Great-uncle Sidney.

In cut they were far from fashionable – I dare say he first wore them while Trollope was still alive – and in colour a kind of rusty black. But the principal trouble stemmed from the fact that Uncle Sid, though I never set eyes upon him, must by comparison with me have been very tall, extremely narrow-chested, and pot-bellied.

Setting off for either of these annual fandangoes was therefore a matter necessitating a particular drill. First, strong safety-pins were needed to draw together behind me the spare material of the overlarge waistband; it did not matter that this left the seat of the trousers puckered into a series of vertical creases like the corrugations of a fan, since all was concealed by the overlong tail-coat. Next, a shortish but strong pair of braces was essential, to hoist the trousers to maximum height and thus to allow at least the soles of my shoes to escape below the endless trouser legs; this in itself rendered the fly buttons useless because of altitude and made the passing of water a major undertaking. And lastly, if I were not to split the ancient cloth of the coat, I needed to make my shoulders no wider than had been Uncle Sid's. This I could only do by rounding my back, keeping my elbows close to one another, and bending always slightly forward, so that all in all I looked like nothing so much as a rather seedy, obsequious footman.

And then there was the problem of transport. The Land Rover is an able vehicle, but in its basic early form not ideally designed for use in the depths of winter when one is tarted up to the nines.

Ours had a canvas hood, which kept out rain but not cold airs, and either no heater or one so inadequate as to be unmemorable. Myrle's dress would thus need insulating with several coats and rugs, and Uncle Sid's regalia was covered by a duffel coat and over that a leather jerkin. Gloves and scarves were *de rigueur*, and hot-water bottles not unknown.

The other practical problem was one of cleanliness. The Land Rover had to be swept clear of calf dung or goat pellets, and the whole of the inside, front as well since the pedals were always plastered in muck, washed out with disinfectant. All we then needed was a couple of paper chickmeal sacks under our feet, and then it was off to the Ball and on to the floor. The hunched style of dancing which Uncle Sid's suit forced upon me was no doubt taken to be an effort to accommodate my height to Myrle's, and no one ever commented on the slight pungency of Jeyes' Fluid.

Hunting people are supposedly weatherproof, and bad conditions like a heavy snowfall never seemed to affect the attendance. But on occasion the gods of the elements had a quiet snigger.

One year the roads were sheeted with black ice by the time that the merrymakers drove away from the great duke's house, and as a convoy of twelve cars came, quite circumspectly, down a nearby hill, the fun began.

The leading driver, all his steering, gear-changing, and braking availing him nought, eventually came, once gravity had done with him, to a broadside stop at the bottom. Into him bumped the second. Solemnly, inexorably, almost in strict tempo, the remaining ten skated into one another in a weird moonlit ballet.

Car number thirteen was being driven by a gallant and distinguished colonel, whose long service to the British Raj had clearly created the man most fitted to unscramble such a scene of chaos. The ability that had solved great problems of military engineering from Calcutta to Kandahar was not likely to have much trouble sorting out a dozen cars in Old Sodbury.

Carefully he stopped short of the mêlée. Taking in the situation with one incisive glance, he got out. Masterfully he strode towards the incompetent fools who had been unable to cope with something as simple as a slippery road.

But even as those crisp words of command rang out, in tones that had reduced sepoys to sobs and jemadars to jelly, they were drowned by a sudden loud crash, as number fourteen smashed the colonel's car to scrap.

Hunt balls, of either persuasion, were on the whole pretty unremarkable. The prevailing characteristic of the dancers was likely to be heartiness, since a good proportion would be what a pair of Gaelic friends always referred to as 'honkers': English persons, that is, usually of the upper-middle classes, given to the public expression of their opinions in very loud voices, and not infrequently capable of a fair degree of unthinking condescension towards lesser mortals. Honkers particularly enjoyed such dances as the Posthorn Gallop, and when in wine favoured such amusements as throwing bread rolls, balancing full glasses on their heads, or, for a good laugh, setting the occasional tablecloth on fire. They would holler unselfconsciously whenever they viewed another of the species, of either sex, across the floor.

We usually made up a party of eight or ten other couples, and were not wholly innocent of honkerishness. Usually plenty of food and exercise kept the effects of drink at bay, and now and again pleasantly uninhibited moments would make the evening one to be remembered, like one particular gathering at the Pump Room.

By supper-time our party had grown by the addition of three total strangers who came to sit with us unasked – a dull girl with a very long double-barrelled name, a man who was introduced as 'Armadillo Dung', and a second man who said nothing but looked ill.

As we all sat eating, strange expressions varying from

pleasure through puzzlement to downright annoyance began to pass over the faces of the women, as each glanced, or studiously did not look, at her neighbour, be he someone else's husband or Armadillo Dung or the unnamed stranger. Beneath the table, the smallest and most sloshed of us was crawling happily round on hands and knees, feeling each and every female leg in turn.

No sooner had he been discovered and hauled out than the face of the nameless man, which had now turned putty-coloured, fell forward with a splash into his plate, and ominous convulsive sounds threatened worse to come. With great presence of mind somebody grabbed a jug of water that stood, surprisingly, among the army of bottles, and emptied it into a pot-plant in time to catch the stranger's sole contribution to the evening.

And to round that night off there were a couple of splendid public rows. One was a case of good old-fashioned jealousy between husband and wife.

'Just how many more times do you intend to dance with so-and-so?'

'As many as I like. If you want to dance with me, you've got a tongue in your head.'

'Bloody disgusting, slobbering all over the bloody man. Everybody's been looking at you.'

'I was not slobbering, as you call it. And everybody's looking at you, shouting and yelling and making an idiot of yourself.'

'I AM NOT SHOUTING ...' And so on.

The other barney was a little more unusual, for the couple were newly engaged and might therefore have been expected to be happy with one another. But suddenly, for whatever cause – and we could not hear above the music the furious words that we could see them spitting as they danced angrily past the band – the girl broke free from her fiancé's grip and tore off her engagement ring. Setting herself like a discus thrower, she hurled it into the midst of the bemused musicians even as they resolutely rendered some sweet song for young lovers.

And after the ball was over and we were muffled and gloved for the cold haul home, we took a last look into the dimmed and deserted ballroom. The stage still held one large shadowy figure, searching on hands and knees for that symbol of happy bondage that was gone with the wind or more probably with the brass, straight down somebody's euphonium.

Memory treasures one last unforgettable picture, at the very end of yet another annual beaglers' assembly, this time at the Guildhall. Coats had all been left somewhere in the upper regions of the building, so that Thomas Baldwin's fine flight of stairs carried a press of people making their way up or down, a way that was unusually narrow by reason of a magnificent display of many-coloured flowers arranged along the length of the staircase.

Suddenly the gaze of the entire company, both those like

us who were gathered in the great hall below already dressed for the journey, and those climbing or descending, was drawn to one of our party, a tall figure standing midway between top and bottom. A steady stream of men and women gingerly edged their way past him, faces rigid in their studied lack of expression.

His customary short 'nose-warmer' pipe was clenched between his teeth, his handsome head was bent in concentration, and he wore the blissful look of the man who is bursting and has made it to the garden at last, as with both hands he carefully directed upon that great bank of chrysanthemums a steady, clearly visible, and seemingly never-ending parabola of pee.

Chapter 12

GOATS, CHILDREN AND DUCKS

14 May
Sunday after Ascension
Drove Rachel to Saanen billy-goat.

Actually the workaday pattern of life was a very sober-coloured one. As a rule we only had a drink proper at weekends. The perfect caveat passed the bottom of the farm drive every morning, in the shape of the tragic-comic figure of Cider Harry, *en route* for The Ring of Bells. During the war, Cider Harry had been that then most respected of rural figures, the local police sergeant. But now, only a handful of years later, the scrumpy had cost him first his stripes and then his job, and made of him a sad figure of fun.

Cider Harry

He always smiled.
It was a fact of course
They like that kind of copper in the force;
Smiling, and six foot, give or take an inch,
And fifteen stone, say sixteen at a pinch;
Benevolent and fatherly and fat,
Face red as fallen crabs.
                            The apple that
Caused Harry's downfall from sobriety
Was of a different variety:
For it was scrumpy that laid down the law.
A dozen pints a day?
                            It could be more.

I don't know why.
                            I mean I don't know why
He drank so hard. Perhaps to damp some dry
Old scar, drown some old love's still frantic clutch,
Or did he simply like the stuff too much?
They took away his stripes and then his job,
For now the smile was fixed.

The odd two bob
From friends kept him in drink. His sister kept
Him in a chicken-house. Quite warm. She swept
It out, removed the perches. "Pon my soul,
Can't have him in with us.

                     He's no control.

He's like a child.
He'll do it in the road.'
And so, where once with dignity he strode,
He shuffles now behind the aimless grin
With silly little steps towards the inn;
Sits in the corner, blink and bow and beam,
Until it's time for bed.

                   You wouldn't dream
How cosy, would you? Close the hen-house door,
Shutters, and pop-hole. Shake the mousy straw.
Feet in the nest-box, pillow is a pile
Of folded chick-meal sacks.

                   See Harry smile.

February 1972

Unbuttoned, unlaced, his face a match for the reddest apple, he grinned his way along the road, his nose a huge squashed strawberry above the slack mouth. He was a big man, but his long stride had turned to a short nervous shuffle, as though he must keep both feet pressed to the ground or, raising one, risk a fall.

Not quite oblivious to the world, for he would nod in answer to a greeting, Cider Harry hurried carefully towards the pub, and then, much later, back home again, this time pausing once or twice to urinate in the hedge, his back politely turned to the passing traffic. Home, they said in the village, was a chicken-house in his sister's garden. She would not have him come indoors.

The memory of Cider Harry has lingered because I named my first goat, perhaps for some reason of resemblance, after his sister, a Mrs Pearce.

My Mrs Pearce was a gentle sweet-natured animal, black-and-white, and carrying a modest pair of neat crenellated horns by which she could be led about without any of that pulling and head-tossing or butting in which some goats indulge.

She was very hairy, not only about the chin, so that a skirt or apron of hair hung about her almost to the ground. She was small, like her milk yield, and short, like her life with us. For when I went to milk poor Mrs Pearce one morning in the orchard, where she was tethered, there she lay with her throat torn out.

There had been some worrying in the district, and one dog, I suppose, could not tell the goats from the sheep.

In due course I acquired a number of goats, but at least had sense enough not to keep a billy. The smell of the one to which I first took my nanny-goat was powerful enough even to have cleared Cider Harry's head. Large and shaggy, with a wicked sweep of horn, this animal was very obviously common in the unkindest sense of the word, compounding its natural rankness by spraying itself with its own urine. Its coat thus more yellow than white, it would advance upon the visiting female, neck outstretched and head thrown back so that the horn tips rested upon its withers. Cold eyes half-closed in anticipation, nostrils flaring, it rolled its rubbery upper lip back from its dirty teeth with a horrid relish.

A nice old superstition says that you never see a goat for the whole of the twenty-four hours, because once every day it pays a visit to the Devil to have its beard combed. After a couple of times I decided never to see this one again, not for one minute, and took my animals in future to an elegant pedigree Saanen who was hornless, practically clean-shaven, and by comparison positively fragrant.

First to wed this upper-class person was my fourth and favourite goat, Rachel. After Mrs Pearce's tragic end, Mrs Wilkins had slipped off a steep bank and strangled herself on her tethering chain, and Mrs Maypole had tired of life and died in her sleep, so I renounced the local ladies and named Rachel for her looks, which were pure Old Testament.

She was an Anglo-Nubian, a breed with large pendulous ears and a profile of Roman nobility. I couldn't find a billy of her own sort within range, but the gentlemanly Saanen was good enough, the object of our goat-keeping being simply to produce milk to feed to dachshund puppies. It didn't matter how the kids turned out. Whatever they looked like, they were a delight to watch as they skipped about the orchard; and when they were old enough we would sell the females and eat the males, another delight, like spring lamb with a hint of venison.

Transport for animals at that time was a large custard-coloured Austin van, once the property of a baker, which I had bought by mistake at a farm sale. Watching disinterestedly as the bidding reached thirty-six pounds, I had chanced to look towards the auctioneer, a friend, who nodded his head at me so I nodded back, and he knocked it down to me.

'Too good to miss,' he said afterwards, and he was right. Twenty years old it may have been, but it served me well for three more until I sold it, for thirty-six pounds.

Driving it was, I imagine, like driving a bus, sitting high above the passing cars and double-declutching my way through the heavy gate-gears. Rachel's first trip in the baker's van was memorable, since she immediately jumped out of the back and sat composedly by me on the front seat, looking down her patrician nose at the foolish humans who laughed and pointed as we went on our stately way to the home of the billy-goat. Suddenly I saw in the distance two elderly acquaintances walking towards us. I whipped off my hat and placed it on Rachel's bony dome. I retain the picture of their startled faces as we swept solemnly past.

We had friends who kept Anglo-Nubians, and passing the bedroom window of their bungalow one day, I noticed with a little surprise that on their double bed there lay side by side three large nannies, sensuous, relaxed, and enigmatic, like Goya's *Naked Maja* in triplicate with a bit of help from Salvador Dali. I knocked on the front door.

'John, do you know there are three goats on your bed?'

'Bloody hell,' he said resignedly, 'not again. Goat pellets are so much worse than biscuit crumbs.'

After Giles was born, Myrle stopped showing the dachshunds and we gave up goat-keeping. But earlier, when regular litters of puppies made the chore of milking goats worthwhile, I was scanning the livestock section of

Exchange & Mart, looking as ever for a bargain, and saw what seemed a cracker:

'Eight young female goats. £4 the lot.'

Hastily I sent off a cheque to an address in Staffordshire. A couple of weeks later I had heard nothing and the money looked to have been wasted. Then the phone rang.

'Mr King-Smith?'

'Yes.'

'Williams here, station master.'

'Oh yes, Mr Williams?'

'Were you expecting some goats?'

'Oh. Yes, I was.'

'Perhaps you'd come up to the station right away. They're all over the line, and the down express is due through in ten minutes.'

When Gladwyn and I arrived in the baker's van, there were seven gaunt goats of unknown ancestry and a variety of colours wandering dispiritedly on the tracks. The eighth the station master held. All were thin as rakes, their ribs like toast-racks, their bleats of protest feeble.

We rounded them up, quite easily, for they had no strength to resist, and shoved them into the van as the express came rushing through.

'When we opened the door of the wagon they came tumbling out,' said Mr Williams. 'The poor sods are starving, they've eaten the string they were tied up with, and even the labels off each other's necks, bar this one.' And he showed me a scrap of cardboard.

'... Smith' it said, and below that '... Farm', and at the bottom the last few letters of the name of the village.

'That's how I knew they were yours.'

They weren't mine for very long, for though I worked hard to rekindle their interest in life, they could not respond. Riddled with worms, they could get no good of the food of which they had been starved, and all died, of their own accord or mine. You gets what you pays for.

For Myrle and me, life at Woodlands Farm was really an extension of our childhood pet-keeping. Breeding animals was the thing we liked doing and in an ideal world we probably wouldn't have sent the calves to market or the piglets to the dealer or the chickens and ducks and rabbits to the deep-freeze, but instead kept the lot, revelling in the increase in our flocks and herds. But of course during the fourteen years we were there, the most important increases were to our own family. We'd arrived with Juliet, aged two. Almost immediately, Betsy had been born. Then, five years later, Giles appeared.

Though he has managed to retain his given name in later life, nicknames are two a penny in my family, and, as 'Gordon' became Dick, so Juliet is usually known as 'Buddy', and Betsy always as 'Liz'.

All three inherited from us the notion that farm animals were all just pets – they treated Monty, for example, as a large sort of dog – and one of their favourites was Snowballs. Snowballs was a duck, or to be more precise a Muscovy drake.

We kept a lot of Muscovies (good eating: the ducks Aylesbury-sized, the drakes much larger, dressing out at seven or eight pounds, the flesh dark and goose-like). Snowballs, pure white, was the grand seigneur of a large harem of females, black-and-white or blue-and-white, and his mission in life was a simple one, namely to pass on his genes.

The mating of Muscovy ducks is a kind of ballet, not only of movement but of noise, not of quacking as with common or garden ducks, but a sound of hissing. The neat female gives quick little gasps as of ecstasy already enjoyed rather than yet to come, while the great drake lets off steam with the regular rasp of a steam locomotive pulling away from the platform. Grotesque he is, this lumbering *premier danseur*, short-legged yet long-bodied, somehow seeming as much goose as duck: adorning his face are bold patches of naked red skin which flame with passion as he treads his measure. Round and round each other they move, heads jerking back and forth like pistons in a stately sibilant *pas de deux*. More often than not, the stage is filled, the entire *corps de ballet* hissing and twitching around the principals as the dance moves to its climax.

There must have been something in the pomp and circumstance of Snowballs' unending attention to duty that fascinated our children. There was nothing of prurience in this. For if you grow up on a farm, you look upon conception, birth, and indeed death with an experienced and level eye. So, often the two girls and Giles would solemnly dance around the courting couple, intoning as they did so some primitive chant of cadenced jingle that blended with the gobbling gasps of the lovers. Beyond the three children, kept at another remove from centre stage, the *corps de ballet* dutifully bowed and bobbed.

But there was at last a morning when the children came rushing to find me. They had been dancing the ritual dance, but this time the ending was different. They led me to that day's stage, a little side-lawn under a false-cherry tree and there he lay, the Prince, flat on his back, his cheek-patches and wattles engorged with purpling blood. His flashing eyes were closed at last, that rasping hiss was silenced, and the mighty emblem of his drakehood lay flaccid and still for ever upon the dirty feathers of his stomach.

'Go, bid the soldiers shoot!'

Chapter 13

A Farmer No More

1 November
All Saints' Day. New Moon.
The end of the road. Dispersal sale.
Big attendance. Lots of bargains.

Though I rate myself as having been a reasonably good stockman, caring properly for my animals, I was (and still am) a hopeless business man. Worse, there was no pressure on me to do better at this so important part of farming, for the Golden Valley Paper Mills didn't much mind if the farm made a loss. They simply set it off against tax. So for fourteen years I failed to record even the most modest profit. Had Myrle looked after the farm accounts, then, and later when we moved to a much bigger farm, things might have been different. She couldn't have been worse than me. But she had the cooking and the housework and all the gardening and the children to look after, and all her breeding and showing of dachshunds.

At last in 1961, the paper mills ceased trading after fifty-three years under first Grampy K-S and then Father. It was one of the very few remaining small family mills, making high-quality paper, and with its outdated machinery, no longer in a position to compete with the big boys in papermaking. So it folded, and then of course Woodlands Farm was put on the market.

What was to become of us? By chance, an old friend of Father's owned a farm a handful of miles away whose tenant was about to retire, and so I was offered the tenancy of Overscourt Farm, at 200 acres four times the size of Woodlands Farm.

I would love (how I would love) to be able to tell you that the six years that I spent as the tenant of Overscourt Farm were, financially, successful. But alas one thing didn't change, namely my lack of business sense. Gone were the pigs and the goats, three times as large as the dairy herd that Gladwyn and I had to milk; I grew a large acreage of corn, and we started out with high hopes. Yet six short years later, I was done for, six years in which Myrle had worked so hard to make the old Elizabethan farmhouse (which needed a lot of money spent on it) into a comfortable home.

There were excuses for me, I suppose. It was, by general agreement, a difficult farm to work, some of it heavy clay, some useless woodland, some thin old pasture. The rent was high, and the man who eventually succeeded me as tenant couldn't make a go of it either. But still it hurt, to have wanted to farm, to have been a farmer for twenty years, and to finish up a failed farmer. The day of the dispersal sale in 1967 was hard to bear, having to watch the stock sold, the cows, the few chickens, the many ducks – all, by selection, pure white now in memory of their great ancestor Snowballs – the machinery, the implements, all passing into the hands of strangers.

We'd had good times at Overscourt Farm as a family, of course we had, and as a family we were happy. But my most abiding memories are of two accidents that happened to me there.

I was always having accidents. Curious that they always seemed to be my fault.

For example, there was an old cart-shed, the roof of which was failing to such an extent that I became afraid it might actually fall on someone, the children perhaps. I determined to engineer its collapse. I tied a rope to a large central A-frame, which I (rightly) considered the keystone to the whole business, prior to going safely outside and pulling. Unfortunately I did just give one sharp tug while still inside – just to make sure the knot was properly tied – and the A-frame promptly fell on my head.

I visited the same hospital not many months later for a different reason. We had a new contrivance for the foreloader of the tractor: a heavy metal scoop, held in place by two steel bolts each the size of a large cigar. We had been shifting some very wet dung, slurry in fact, and when the job was finished, I set about disconnecting the scoop. Obviously these bolts had to come out, so I pushed one of them through with my forefinger and the whole weight of the five-hundredweight bucket fell on it.

Doubtless there are even less pleasant situations than to squirm on your belly in liquid manure with your finger trapped in a foreloader scoop, but my agony would have been even longer had it not been for Tom's presence of mind. Tom had replaced Gladwyn as my cowman, though in fact I did most of the milking to leave him free to do those mechanical jobs at which, not understanding machinery, I wasn't much good. Finding that his efforts to lift off the weight were unavailing and merely incited me to louder shouts of pain, he leaped into the driving seat of the tractor, started the engine, engaged the hydraulic lift, and very gently, very slowly (for too rapid a rise would simply have chopped my finger off) eased up the scoop till I could pull free.

Myrle drove me straight in to casualty, filthy and stinking as I was. Damage to one's extremities is especially painful, but through my anguish I still noticed that everyone stood up and moved away, leaving me sitting all by myself. After a while the sister came in with a large aerosol. Ah, pain-killer, I thought. As she sprayed it liberally on and about me, I saw the label on the can. It said 'Spring Violets'.

What a strange awakening there was for me on that first morning after the dispersal sale. No cows to milk. After twenty years, no need to get up at the crack of dawn. But what were we to do? Where were we to go? The first stroke of luck was that a friend called Anne had moved out of her cottage, intending to sell it, but seeing our plight, offered it to us to live in for the time being, rent free. We had somewhere to go. Then came the next stroke of luck when along came another friend, Pat. He offered me a job, a temporary job, for six months only, but it meant that I had something to do and got me off the dole. Pat manufactured, among other sorts of clothing, special fire-fighting suits made from aluminized asbestos and guaranteed to withstand very high temperatures. So now I became a rep, a travelling salesman driving all about

England, to airfields, to motor-racing tracks, to petro-chemical works, trying to sell aluminized asbestos fire-fighting suits, boots and helmets.

I had to use my own car (and the mileage I covered pretty well wore it out) but Pat paid for the petrol and I stayed in a good many rather nice hotels at his expense. I quite enjoyed myself, seeing bits of England I'd never seen before, but it was no fun at all for Myrle, stuck on her own in the borrowed cottage all week.

The one thing that I was terrified of was that on one of my visits, someone would say to me, 'So this suit will protect the wearer in a really hot fire, will it?'

'Oh yes! Up to one thousand degrees centigrade.'

'Good, because we've built a nice big bonfire all ready for you. We'll light it now and when you're all dressed up, you can walk into it.'

Mercifully, no one ever did this. At the end of my six months as a rep (I did sell a few of the fire-fighting suits but nothing like as many as a professional salesman would have done), there I was, back on the dole again.

For the next three and a bit years I worked in a shoe factory, a job that I landed through the kindness of another friend, David. I was a work-study engineer, a posh name for a time-and-motion man, but having to drive into Bristol each day and walk about the factory floor dressed in a white coat and carrying stopwatch and clipboard was something, I found, that I could only take for so long. I resigned, just in time – I'm sure they were about to sack me.

So, I was on the dole for the third time. First, as failed farmer. Next, as time-expired salesman of aluminized asbestos fire-fighting suits, boots and helmets. Now, as ex-work-study engineer.

So – what to do? I was only forty-nine. I had no private means. I needed an income. Someone suggested teaching. But I'd need qualifications. My only academic achievements were credits in the school certificate, thirty-three years ago.

Along comes another piece of good fortune. An old friend, Charles, was in turn a friend of someone who was a tutor at a teacher-training establishment, the College of St Matthias in Bristol. Charles brought the man to see me, and I was given an interview, and, in the nick of time, got a place on the impending three-year course, and a grant. The grant was not generous but Father topped it up a little, and so now I found myself, at the ripe old age of forty-nine, being taught to be a teacher.

Best of all, at last we had a real home of our own. We found a very old, very small cottage in a little village (no more than three miles as the crow flies from the house in which I'd been born) and were lucky enough to buy it at auction. Early in the summer of 1968 we moved in. And, as she had done at Overscourt Farm, Myrle set about putting the inside of the cottage to rights, painting and decorating and – hardest of all – painstakingly removing from the good old oak beams the layers of paint that had been slapped on them.

It was all fun, those three years as an elderly student, so much so that I determined, with Myrle's approval, to stay on for a fourth year, in order to gain a degree in education from Bristol University. Which I duly did. So there I was (it's 1975 now), a qualified teacher with no one to teach. By now I knew the sort of job I wanted. One, it had to be near home – I didn't want to have to drive miles to work for years and years. Two, it must be in a country school. Three, it must be in the primary sector – I didn't want to have to deal with people over the age of puberty.

Once again, fortune smiled. I had an interview, just one, at a village primary school five miles from my door, and as I drove back down the lane to our cottage, there was Myrle, in the garden, eyebrows raised high in hopeful query. Happily, I stuck my thumb up.

I taught at Farmborough Primary School for seven years, that is to say from age fifty-three to age sixty. Part of the school was very old, built in 1857. Part was brand spanking new. For four years I taught eight-year-olds, in one of the new classrooms. For the final three years I taught six-year-olds in one of the old classrooms, its walls crying out for a lick of paint, its roof so leaky that in a real downpour, bowls were needed on the floor at strategic points to catch the drips. But actually I preferred the old classroom because I was happier in it, and thereby hangs a tale.

My headmistress, a woman about the age of my elder daughter, became, understandably, worried at the end of my first four years. Not because I was the only male teacher, but because my problems with understanding maths were not helping my pupils.

She decided to move me from the juniors to the infants, presumably on the basis that though I couldn't understand long division, I could just about add two to three to make five. So then I had three good years with those young ones and very rewarding I found them. Many years later I wrote a book (*The Schoolmouse*) set in that very classroom.

Being the only man in the school, I was also in charge of football, as coach (not a very good one) and, at school matches, as referee (weak on the offside law).

But all this time I had not only been teaching, but also writing. In the summer holidays of 1976 – when I should have spent my time preparing next year's classroom work – I wrote my very first attempt at a children's book.

I'd had the ideas for it twenty years earlier in the middle of the farming era, when that passing fox had murdered a whole lot of my chickens. One day, I said to myself, I'll have a go at writing a story where the weak are victorious over the strong, where the chickens vanquish the foxes.

So long had the notion been in my mind that I actually wrote the first draft of *The Fox Busters* in three weeks. The first two publishers to whom I sent the manuscript rejected it, though with polite notes (both houses published me later, I'm glad to say), but the third, Victor Gollancz, actually expressed a deal of interest in the story, thanks to a wonderful editor, name of Jo. She pushed me and pulled me and bullied me and encouraged me, until at last I knocked the story into publishable shape. I owe Jo a great deal.

When first you learn to ride a bike, you fall off quite a lot, and the same goes for learning anything quite new, like writing books for children. I had some false starts and made a lot of booboos, but in fact I found I was reasonably well equipped. I'd had a good education, at my prep school and at my public school, at both of which I'd been taught Latin and Greek, languages that teach you a lot about words. I love words (just as I hate numbers), and had always written a lot of verse, though never before had I attempted a children's story.

I've written well over a hundred books now, mostly about animals, and there I had a lot going for me, the boyhood pet-keeping (and not only boyhood, I had loads of guinea-pigs in my fifties) and of course the twenty years of farming. Also I found, once I'd buckled down to the job, that I had masses of ideas for stories and that I was getting a whole lot of fun writing them.

My first sight of *The Fox Busters* in a Bristol bookshop excited me no end, and I said to myself that now I was a published children's author, no doubt they would welcome a second book. I set to work on a zoo story, its hero a sparrow named Riff-Raff.

Jo's response to it was lukewarm. 'It's not terribly exciting, is it?'

I responded by a rewrite, which I made incredibly bloodthirsty.

'I can't publish this,' she wrote. 'It's far too bloodthirsty.'

Undeterred, I produced my first pig story, *Daggie Dogfoot*.

'This is more like it,' said Jo. 'But it's far too long, it's about forty-five thousand words. I don't want more than twenty-five thousand at the most.'

Stupid woman, I thought, losing all those words will ruin the thing. But it didn't of course, it was the making of it, because it tightened the whole book up and kept the pace of it going, and she published it.

The *Fox Busters* was published in 1978. Then followed *Daggie Dogfoot* (1980). *The Mouse Butcher* (1981) and *Magnus Powermouse* (1982), all written during my time at Farmborough Primary School, which time was soon to come to an end. Teaching children was to give way to writing books for children.

I wasn't ass enough to think I could make a living as a

children's author – only the Dahls of this world did that – but Myrle and I worked out (with help from a financial adviser) that it should be possible for me to give up teaching and try my luck as an author.

Chapter 14

A Little TV, a Lot of Books

 *'That'll do,' said Farmer Hogget to his sheep-pig. 'That'll do.'*

Now began for me a new full-time career, where I hadn't to go out to work, but simply climb the stairs to my study, get paper and pen, and write and write and write. Yet another piece of luck came along with perfect timing. For, sadly, both my parents died in 1980, and, thanks to money that they left me, we were able in 1982 to build an extension on to the cottage that itself had been built, we were told, round about 1635.

For years we'd had to put up with a lean-to bathroom and loo next to the sitting-room. Now the plan was to build a new upstairs bathroom on top of a new downstairs dining room, and by great good luck there was just room to make a very small study for me beside the new bathroom. (I'm writing in it today and I can touch the walls on either side of my chair without straightening my arms.)

I write in all the wrong ways. I don't plan a story out as I should, I just get an idea and blast off into the wild blue yonder, hoping that things will turn out OK and that it will eventually have what all successful stories must have, whether they be for children or adults, namely a Good Beginning, a Good Middle and a Good End. Usually it works, sometimes it doesn't, but it suits me.

In the mornings I scribble away with a pen on rough paper (in fact I use the back sides of old letters – Granny K-S would approve). The handwriting is awful, there are arrows and crossings-out and asterisks and additions in red ink or green: if I died one lunchtime, Myrle wouldn't have a clue what I'd written. Ah, but then in the afternoon I get out my little old portable typewriter and with the index finger of my right hand, I carefully type out the morning's work.

In the evening, if I've written enough, a chapter, say, I read it to my wife. If she says 'Super' or 'Great' or some such, that's grand. If she says 'Yes, well, I think it's time I put the Brussels sprouts on,' and appears less than impressed by what I've read, I have to begin thinking very seriously. Is this story going wrong? How is it going wrong? Is it just a load of rubbish? Sometimes it is.

The great thing about my very slow method of putting words on paper is that it gives me plenty of time to edit myself as I go along. I don't want to do any more one-fingered typing than I have to.

So now, apart from helping Myrle in the garden (lawn-mowing, weeding, etc, leaving the clever stuff to her) and our daily walks with the dogs, I sat in my new study writing away, and the books began to spring up like mushrooms. *The Queen's Nose* (1983) was my fifth book and *Harry's Mad* (1984) my seventh, but in between them came book number six, also published in 1983, which, had I known it, was probably to be for me the most successful of all the 100 plus children's books that I've written.

That book was *The Sheep-Pig*, which to my surprise and delight won the *Guardian* Award for Children's Literature (£250 – I bought an armchair with it, in which I still sit very comfortably). How amazed I would have been at the idea that a dozen years later *The Sheep-Pig* was to become the film *Babe*, which had such worldwide success.

The first ten books that I wrote were all published by Victor Gollancz, but by now I was going at such a rate (seven or eight titles per year) that no single publishing house could hold me: and as well as the hardbacks, everything was coming out in paperback too, principally in Puffin.

For Walker Books, I wrote a series of stories – six books in all – about a small but very determined little girl called Sophie. Children often ask me who Sophie was based on. The answer is Myrle, even though I hadn't known her until she was fourteen. But in most respects, Sophie was made to resemble her, and Sophie's great friend, her Great-great-aunt Alice, was squarely based on my own Great-aunt Al.

A large number of my books rely heavily upon anthropomorphism. Big word, eh? Derived from ancient Greek (*anthropos* – man, *morphe* – shape) it simply means that someone like me is giving certain human characteristics to what is not human, namely an animal.

Much use has always been made of it in children's literature. One thinks of the authors of some of the classic books – Kipling writing *The Jungle Book*. Beatrix Potter and her rabbits and squirrels and mice, Kenneth Grahame and *The Wind in the Willows*. Unlike the last two mentioned, I don't dress my animal characters up in human clothes, but I do make use of the anthropomorphic tradition to give them certain human characteristics that they might not possess in real life, such as courage in the face of adversity, determination in the face of difficulties (Babe routing the sheep-worrying dogs, Flora in *The Schoolmouse* teaching herself to read).

Above all else, I can give them the power to speak, to use the English language to convey their thoughts, their reactions, their sense of humour, their relationships.

It's a very thin tightrope to walk, is anthropomorphism. I just hope that I, mostly, don't fall off.

Some animals, of course, do talk, and I am reminded of two particular individuals that once belonged to members of my family. The first was an African Grey parrot, by the somewhat banal name of Polly, owned by my Uncle Alan. Polly only ever said two words of the English language but he (she?) said them each morning as my uncle came downstairs.

From the cage in the hall Polly would say loudly, 'Morning, Al!'

'Good morning, Polly,' would come the answer.

But one morning, greeting came there none. The bird was lying on the floor of the cage, legs in the air, having had some kind of a stroke.

My uncle agonized about what to do. Polly needed to be given a merciful death, but you can't wring the neck of someone who has lived with you for forty years. So, after much thought, Uncle Alan went back upstairs, found an empty shoe-box, put the unconscious parrot in it, put the lid back on, put the box out in the middle of the lawn, fetched his shotgun, and shot the shoe-box.

The second talker was a green budgerigar belonging to

my cousin Helen Bingham. He too was economical in his use of language, for all he ever said was, 'My name is Charlie Bingham.'

Once windows and doors were closed, Charlie was allowed to fly free about Helen's living room, a privilege that led to his demise on the day when a visitor brought a nippy little terrier to the house. My cousin managed to rescue the bird from the dog's jaws, and as she cradled his mortally injured form in her hands, he looked up at her and whispered, 'My … name … is … Charlie … Bingham,' and died.

When I was in the doldrums, I was lucky enough, as I've said, to have had friends to help me.

Now that at last I was sailing with a fair wind, I was fortunate – and still am – to have my friend Michael as my accountant. He lives opposite to me, just across the lane, so that when I forget to bring him the correct papers or accounts which he needs (for I'm still just as unbusiness-like as I was in the farming days), why, it doesn't take a minute to pop back and fetch them.

There is one more mini-career that came along with my new status as a children's author, and that was on the television. In the early Eighties, Anne Wood, now famous as the creator of the *Teletubbies*, was producing a Sunday morning children's programme called *Rub-a-dub-tub*, and she was looking for someone to present a spot on it about animals. She was looking in fact for someone who had been a farmer, who had been a teacher, who wrote books for children and who owned a small photogenic dog. I fitted that bill, along with our wire-haired miniature dachshund – Dodo. Was I interested? I was!

All through our life together Myrle and I have had masses of dogs – German Shepherds, Great Danes, terriers and dachshunds. Of them all, Dodo was the one designed for stardom. She loved the camera, she loved the crew, she knew exactly when they usually came to the cottage (9.00 a.m. on a Thursday morning) and she'd be waiting by the door, at that time, on that day. Dodo had always been very self-possessed. When we brought her home as a puppy, we put her down on the lawn to be introduced to Daniel, our current Great Dane. He bent his great head towards this tiny creature, and she wagged happily at him.

I was much looking forward to being a presenter on TV (in a very small way, mind you) and I thought, being naturally a bit of a show-off, that I'd be good at the job. But the first time I had to speak to camera, I became completely wooden. Confronted with this metal box, I found it difficult to be natural. Anne came to the rescue.

'Who's your youngest grandchild?' she asked.

'Charlie.'

'Right then, just imagine that Charlie is inside that metal box. Talk to him as if he were.' And it worked. Gradually – it took time – I learned to perform on TV in a reasonably successful way. At first, in my little slot on *Rub-a-dub-tub*, we concentrated on moo-cows and baa-lambs and piggy-wigs, but gradually, as we made more and more little programmes (over fifty in all, I should think), Dodo and I would be filmed with all sorts of creatures, from badger cubs to birds of prey, and to exotic animals, like white tigers and pythons.

Dodo was not happy to have a tiger's huge face (dribbling slightly) only six inches from her own, even if there was a stout wire fence between them. And I was rather relieved to be rid of a python called Eric. Eric was not a huge snake, only about ten feet long, but he weighed very heavy, and after I had worn him round my neck like a scarf for half an hour, I began to get tired and Eric began to get bored and started to squeeze me a bit, so I handed him back to his keeper.

Dodo and I were filmed with dozens of different sorts of animals, including, I'm glad to say, two pigs. Bought specially for the programme, they were Gloucester Old Spots, and – because I hadn't room – they lived just across the road in an outhouse of Michael's. After a competition where child viewers were invited to submit names for them, we chose Victoria and Albert, and I'm happy to say they went to a good home once their days of stardom were over.

Then *Rub-a-dub-tub* came to an end, and it looked as though my days as the humblest sort of television presenter were over. But no, Anne had another children's programme in the making, for Channel 4, called *Pob's Programme*.

Pob was a puppet, at whose behest I was given in each episode a clue – such as one would get in a treasure hunt – and was then expected to find something, a place, a thing, an animal, at the end, assisted once again by a dog, though this time not Dodo. Our treasure-hunting entailed climbing steep places and forcing a way through bramble-bushes and sloshing about in muddy wallows – none of which would have appealed to Dodo in the slightest, but were very popular with my brother Tony's dog, Hattie. Hattie was a black Labrador, and the highlight of her television career was when she was required to run down a bank and take an almighty leap into the River Avon; lovely fun.

Was there to be life on TV for me after *Pob*? Yes, and once again for Dodo too, because we went to work for Yorkshire TV to make a series for young children called *Tumbledown Farm*. This was all shot in Yorkshire, at a Rare Breeds Survival Centre called Temple Newsam. Incidentally, I was never recognized as we travelled from Bristol to Leeds, but on one journey the ticket collector stopped dead in his tracks, pointed with a wondering finger at my dog, and said, 'Ee! If it isn't Dodo!'

There were three 'actors' in *Tumbledown Farm* – me, Dodo, and a small girl called Sally Walsh who was posing as my granddaughter. Each episode comprised of three sections. First, there was a set in a big barn where Sally (or 'Georgina' as she now was) interacted with a number of brilliantly handled puppets – chickens, a cat, a rat. Then Georgina and I would be filmed going round the live animals of the centre – pigs, horses, cattle, poultry. And finally we were filmed sitting by the fire in the bothy – a room kept, many years ago, for the farm servants – where I would tell Georgina a story, while Dodo dozed happily before a good fire.

We did two thirteen-part series of *Tumbledown Farm*, and it was very well received; in fact it won some sort of award. But then suddenly it was all over. The powers that be had expected a viewing audience of four million, but got only two million (the figures may not be exact, but you get the point – if you don't reach your target viewing figures, you're out). So ended my brief and very small-scale television career, but I did enjoy it, and so did Dodo.

She's long dead now, as are her daughter, Poppy, and her granddaughter, Little Elsie, and all the many dogs, the dachshunds, the Danes, the terriers, the German Shepherds that Myrle and I have kept over the years. That's the trouble with keeping dogs, isn't it? Like people, they grow old and then they die, but they do it much quicker than people do.

My little career in television may have been over, but the books kept coming and they sold well, and so for the first time in our lives we were comfortably off and didn't have continually to wonder how we were going to pay the bills.

One morning we were out walking with Maggie, the terrier of those days, and two or three dachshunds and, as we came down a field on our way home, Myrle said, 'We haven't had a holiday for ages and ages. We can afford a decent one now. We could go abroad.'

'You're not getting me on a bloody aeroplane,' I said. Horrible things, they're always crashing. I'm scared stiff of them.

'We don't have to fly,' she said. 'We could go by ship. On a cruise.'

A couple of hours later, I was down at the travel agent's, booking a cruise to the Caribbean.

Over the past ten years we've been on about a dozen cruises, sometimes to the Mediterranean, sometimes to the West Indies. But the one that stands out in memory was the maiden world cruise of the P&O liner *Oriana*, three months in all, westwards across the Atlantic, through the Panama Canal, to San Francisco, to New Zealand, to Australia, to Japan (stopping at lots of different islands *en route*) then, with many more ports of call on our way, through the Suez Canal, and so eventually back to Southampton, where almost our entire family was waiting to give us a surprise greeting.

The film *Babe* was now on the screens of the world, and – before we left on the world cruise – the director of the film, an Australian named Chris Noonan, who was on holiday in England, was visiting some old friends in Bristol, and came out to see us.

'When you get to Sydney,' he said, 'I'll meet you and drive you down to the Southern Highlands of New South Wales and show you the location where the film was shot.'

A couple of months later, as the *Oriana* neared Sydney,

a fax was delivered to our cabin. It said: 'Meet you dockside Sydney 11 a.m. Sunday. Chris.'

Ten minutes later, another fax arrived. It said: 'Meet you dockside Sydney 11 a.m. Sunday. Bill.'

This was that same Grenadier, now in his eightieth year, who had been my platoon sergeant and saved my life on 12 July 1944, and had emigrated to Australia in the 1970s. Hastily I had to fax him back, asking if we could meet on the Monday evening instead, because on the Sunday Myrle and I were being driven to the *Babe* location, and on the Monday morning Chris and I were to be interviewed on some TV chat show (it was fun, they had a pen of pigs in the studio).

The location itself was fascinating, chosen precisely because it had rolling countryside (very English-looking) across which they'd built some drystone walls, and because that particular area, which was the site of ancient rainforest, had no (very Australian-looking) gum trees, but only hardwoods.

At all events, it wasn't till the Monday evening that I met Bill Grandfield and his wife Dorothy. Bill was waiting on the quayside, tall, upright, the regimental buttons on his boating-jacket blazing with polish, dazzlingly white shirt, Brigade tie, trousers with a knife-edge crease, shoes you could have shaved in. I was wearing jeans and an old T-shirt and deck shoes ('that baggy officer'). Not until we were seated in a nearby pub did I learn that Bill and Dorothy had travelled nine hours by train to meet me.

On our cruises we visited so many different places in so many different countries, and saw some wonderful things. But one little incident, involving one huge creature, stands out in my memory.

The ship was at anchor at Oahu in the Hawaiian islands, and, sitting out on the balcony of our cabin we could see, perhaps three-quarters of a mile away, a number of whales. Humpback whales they were, that come down from the North in February to spend their mating season in warmer waters. Through binoculars we could see them surfacing to 'blow', and also doing what is known as 'lobtailing' – raising their great tail flukes high out of the water to smack them down again on the surface with a mighty splash.

Suddenly, right beneath us as we sat, a huge humpback whale surfaced so close that we could have dropped an apple, say, down either of its twin blow-holes. Slowly, lazily, it moved away from us, and lifted one great pale paddle-shaped fin high out of the water and slapped it down again. Then it rolled, and did the same with the opposite fin. Then it sank from sight. We felt that it had come to say to us, 'Hullo, I am your personal humpback whale. Greetings!'

Of all the animals that either of us had ever seen, this was by far the biggest.

Now for the first time in our long married life, we don't have any animals, not even a dog. Mind you, next-door's cat – a beautiful little black queen with a white tip to her tail – comes round each day for a second breakfast (and I learned recently that she then goes round to the neighbour on the other side for a third one). But our lives, from when we were both small, have always been filled with animals of one sort or another. Which is why, I dare say, I write so many stories for children about animals.

And do you know the nicest thing for me about this, my last career, as an author? It isn't the money, though it's very pleasant at last not to have to worry – as we used to have to do – about how to pay the bills, and it's good to be able to help our children when they need it. No, the nicest thing for me is the thousands of letters that I get from children, all over the world, who take the trouble to write and tell me that they've enjoyed my books. Sometimes too a mother or a teacher will write to say that Jack or Jill was not really interested in reading, until he, or she, was turned on by one of my stories. That's very rewarding.

And of course every fan letter gets an answer (except for the ones without addresses!). So here I am, in my little study in my old cottage in this new millennium, still writing away happily.

I wasn't a particularly good soldier or farmer or salesman or factory worker or teacher, but at last I've found something I can do reasonably well. I'm a lucky man, in my three children, in all my grandchildren and great-grandchildren, and most especially of course in my wife, who's always backed me up and seen us through bad patches. Without Myrle, I could never have been what I now am.

Looking back at my life so far, there's only one thing to be said, in just the same quiet tones of satisfaction that Farmer Hogget used, at the end of the Grand Challenge Sheep-dog Trials: 'That'll do.'

Dick King-Smith
with Babe & friends
Harry Horse
2000